D0630055

EL ALAMEIN
1942

PIER PAOLO BATTISTELLI

First published 2011
by Spellmount, an imprint of
The History Press
The Mill, Brimscombe Port
Stroud, Gloucestershire, GL5 2QG
www.thehistorypress.co.uk

British Library Cataloguing in Publication Data.
A catalogue record for this book is available from the British Library.

ISBN 978 0 7524 6202 8

Typesetting and origination by The History Press
Printed in Malta
Manufacturing managed by Jellyfish Print Solutions Ltd

CONTENTS

ACKNOWLEDGEMENTS

The author wishes to thank Dr Christopher Pugsley, Royal Military Academy Sandhurst, and the series editor Jo de Vries for their help. Thanks also to the following for their help in securing sources and photos: Lieutenant Colonel Filippo Cappellano (Rome), Professor Piero Crociani (Rome), Dr Andrea Molinari (Milan), Count Ernesto G. Vitetti (Rome).

LIST OF ILLUSTRATIONS

40 A Crusader tank damaged and abandoned.
41 A Blenheim light bomber flying low over a British motorised column in the desert.
42 Tanks burning in front of the wire marking Rommel's 'devil's garden' of mined boxes on the Alamein defence line.
43 German General von Thoma.
44 An infantry squad in the desert, all wearing the khaki drill shirts and shorts.
45 Eighth Army's soldiers capture the crew of a German Panzer III tank in the desert.
46 A destroyed Italian medium tank in the desert.
47 A German 20mm anti-aircraft gun mounted on a British 15cwt Bedford lorry.
48 Rommel with a group of Italian and German officers.
49 Field Marshal Bernard Law Montgomery, Viscount of El Alamein, posing after the war in front of the relic of an Italian tank.
50 Marching past the wire.

Front cover: A Crusader tank of 7th Armoured Division. Perched on top the soldiers include: Ted Fogg, Jack Gadsden, Cyril Livings, Mick Savage, Sep Houghton and Phil Titheridge. Courtesy of Roger Fogg, *The Desert Rats Scrapbook* (The History Press, 2010)

INTRODUCTION

The Mediterranean and the Middle East were only to become theatres of war in June 1940, following Italy's declaration of war against France and Great Britain, and shortly before the fall of France. The strategic situation in Europe during the summer and autumn of 1940 would greatly influence events in these theatres: the German threat against the British Isles and Italy's thrust towards the Balkans largely reduced any interest in both the Mediterranean and the Middle East, where a sideshow war was fought until December of the same year.

The Italian forces, numerically stronger than their enemy, although lacking any suitable degree of motorisation, were to miss countless opportunities to advance into Egypt and seize the delta area, whose control would have changed the fortunes of the war. Only a few months after the German threat against the British Isles disappeared, Britain was able to intervene in the Middle East in an attempt to change the situation.

The offensive started in December 1940 by General Richard O'Connor led to the destruction of a portion of the Italian Army and the seizure of the eastern half of Libya, Cyrenaica – directly threatening Tripoli. This was, seen from the other side, a strategic goal comparable to the seizure of the Nile delta; in either case, one side might have prevailed over the other, thus bringing to an end the whole campaign. In fact, either the Nile delta for the Axis powers or Tripoli for the British were, with their large harbours, the main source for reinforcements, new units, men, weapons and materiel, and all the vital supplies needed to wage a war. Their seizure would have deprived the enemy of every resource, while, on the other hand, by controlling them both sides could feed new forces into the war. Basically, the occupation of these key positions was the reason that no side was able to gain the upper hand, other than temporarily, and to seize a decisive victory.

This is precisely what happened during the following months; in February 1941 the first units of what would have been the Deutsches Afrika Korps, the German corps in Africa, arrived at Tripoli. Meanwhile, the threat of a German intervention in the Italo–Greek war temporarily shifted British attention toward the Balkans, resulting in a new phase of the war in the Western Desert. In April 1941 German and Italian forces, led by the still largely unknown General Erwin Rommel, attacked and seized back the whole of Cyrenaica – apart from the key position of Tobruk (the largest harbour in Cyrenaica), the control of which would have shortened the Axis' supply lines. At the same time, events taking place elsewhere gave a definitive shape to the Mediterranean and Middle Eastern theatres: German seizure of the Balkans in April, followed by the seizure of the island of Crete in May, put an end to the last British foothold in Europe. This made the Middle East, and the Western Desert in particular, the last land theatre of the war where Britain could face Germany and Italy, the latter also being primarily involved in it because of her ambitions to become the only Mediterranean power. The German invasion of the Soviet Union in June turned, from a German point of view, the Mediterranean and the Middle East into secondary theatres of war.

These were the main factors that, from the spring of 1941, dominated the war in the Western Desert. This was a war fought in a rather limited area, stretching from the easternmost region of the Italian colony of Libya, Cyrenaica, to the westernmost part of Egypt; at first down to Sidi Barrani, then to El Alamein (since the Allied landings in the French North-West Africa in November 1942 the Western Desert became the North African campaign). The terrain, mostly sand desert with a few towns along the coast (usually harbours), was another peculiarity of the campaign since, lacking any major feature like rivers or other natural obstacles, it offered unique possibilities to modern motorised and mechanised warfare. These were, however, greatly hampered by the climate, dominated by intense heat during the day and cold at night, and the lack of communications, which made supplies of every kind more essential than ever.

Supplies were, at least from the Axis side, another vital factor; with the desert lacking everything, all materiel was to be brought in from Europe across the Mediterranean. The naval and air battles fought in this area, mainly focusing on Malta, were likewise vital; if Britain succeeded in cutting the sea lanes, then a shortage of supplies would have weakened the Axis forces. Also, the sheer length of the land, with supply lines running from the main harbours to the battlefront, also influenced the situation; the Axis forces did not have access to a railroad, so goods had to be moved using trucks, which consumed their precious fuel. This is why Tobruk, the largest harbour of Cyrenaica close to the Egyptian frontier, became so important. For months, since Rommel's forces besieged it in April 1941 to its eventual seizure in June 1942, this was to be the cornerstone of the Western Desert campaign, a campaign which had already seen many lost opportunities and would see more in the months to follow.

For this was yet another factor of the war in the Western Desert; a decisive victory here, like the one General O'Connor came close to, would have opened a whole series of strategic opportunities. Whereas the kind of sideshow war that was actually fought (because of the many restraints on all sides) during these months only led to seesawing victories and defeats, none proving decisive. Then Rommel's invasion of Egypt in

June 1942 was halted at the El Alamein line (named after a small railway station), creating a kind of a bottleneck squeezed between the Arab Gulf and the Qattara Depression, and as such establishing the last suitable defence line before Alexandria. Rommel's failure to break through the British defences led to a stalemate and created the premise of the last, decisive battle of the Western Desert campaign.

1. The first units of the German Afrika Korps arriving at Tripoli harbour in February 1941, after the Italian defeat at Beda Fomm.

TIMELINE

1940

10 June	Italy declares war on France and Great Britain
13 September	Italian offensive into Egypt, to halt at Sidi Barrani on the 18th
9 December	British Western Desert Force, led by General Richard O'Connor, attacks the Italian positions at Sidi Barrani (Operation Compass), this turns into a major offensive leading to the seizure of Cyrenaica

1941

February	British victory at Beda Fomm and destruction of the Italian Tenth Army; arrival of the first German units in Libya along with their commander, General Erwin Rommel
1 April	Rommel starts his offensive, which leads to the recapture of Cyrenaica
11 April	Tobruk, held by Australian troops, is besieged by the Axis forces, who are unable to seize it, despite repeated attempts
18 November	British Eighth Army's 'Crusader' offensive is started, Tobruk is relieved and on 8 December Rommel's Panzer Army Africa starts to withdraw west

Timeline

1942

21 January	Rommel's second offensive in Cyrenaica, halted at the Gazala line on 4 February
27 May	Panzer Army Africa attacks the Gazala line, and although the plan turns into a failure the following day it eventually defeats the Eighth Army which, on 14 June, starts withdrawing east leaving Tobruk to be held by the South Africans
20–21 June	Tobruk is seized by Panzer Army Africa, which two days later crosses the Libyan–Egyptian frontier
25–28 June	Panzer Army Africa attacks and seizes Mersa Matruh, two days later the forces of the Eighth Army withdraw behind the El Alamein line
1–3 July	First battle of El Alamein: Panzer Army Africa attacks the defence perimeter, but is repulsed by the Eighth Army
9 July	Rommel's second attack against the Alamein line in the south, at Bab el Qattara, fails again
10–14 July	9th Australian and 1st South African divisions attack from the Alamein perimeter
15–17 July	The New Zealand Division attacks at Ruwesait Ridge
21–27 July	Panzer Army Africa faces a serious crisis, although it manages to hold the line; a new series of attacks is launched by Australian, South African and New Zealand forces at Ruwesait and Miteirya ridges; eventually both sides start to dig and form a defence line
12 August	General Bernard Law Montgomery takes over command of the Eighth Army from General Claude Auchinleck

1942

31 August–4 September	Rommel's second attempt to break through the Alamein line, this time moving from the south. The battle of Alam Halfa ends with Panzer Army Africa's failure, and its eventual retreat back to the starting positions. Both sides prepare for the decisive battle
23 September	Rommel leaves Egypt and returns to Germany; temporary command of the Panzer Army Africa is taken over by General Georg Stumme
23 October	Operation Lightfoot: the first phase of the second battle of El Alamein starts
24–26 October	After the attack fails to break through the Panzer Army Africa defences, the 'dog fight' ensues
26–27 October	British 1st Armoured Division attacks Kidney Ridge and repulses Afrika Korps' counterattacks
28–30 October	9th Australian Division swings north and attacks toward the coast, facing fierce opposition from Afrika Korps
1 November	Montgomery devises the Supercharge plan, intended to achieve a decisive breakthrough
2–3 November	Eighth Army starts Operation Supercharge and penetrates the enemy defences, after its counterattacks ended in a failure
4 November	Panzer Army Africa starts its withdrawal to the west
5–6 November	Panzer Army Africa regroups at Fuka before withdrawing further westwards
8 November	Allied landings in French North-West Africa, followed by the Axis creation of the bridgehead at Tunis

Timeline

1942

10–11 November	Panzer Army Africa reaches the Libyan–Egyptian frontier, only to continue with its march to the west
24 November	The Axis forces take position on the Mersa Brega line, which is held until 12 December when Panzer Army Africa starts the second phase of its withdrawal
19 December–15 January	Rommel's last stand on the Buerat line is threatened by Eighth Army's advance and is abandoned on 16 January
23 January	Tripoli is seized by the Allies three months after the beginning of the second battle of El Alamein; the following day the Axis forces start to cross the Libyan–Tunisian frontier
4–15 February	The Axis forces start to deploy on the Mareth line in Tunisia; the war in the Western Desert is over

1943

23 February	Rommel takes over command of the newly formed Army Group Africa; the Panzer Army Africa (also known as German-Italian Panzer Army) becomes 1st Italian Army
14–25 February	Led by Rommel, the Axis attack the US II Corps' positions at Kasserine but fail to achieve a breakthrough
9 March	Rommel leaves North Africa
20–27 March	Battle of the Mareth line, followed by the Axis withdrawal
5–6 April	Battle of Wadi Akarit, the Axis forces retreat into the Tunis bridgehead
19 April–13 May	Last Allied offensive in Tunisia, which ends with the final surrender of all the Axis forces in North Africa

HISTORICAL BACKGROUND

A Crossroad of Strategic Opportunities

Means and ends would eventually make the difference in the Mediterranean and North African theatres of the war, all too often meaning that opportunities were lost while both theatres turned into some kind of a sideshow to the main events in Europe. Italy, protruding into the Mediterranean and with her European borders closed by the barrier of mountains, should have had her main operational areas in both the Mediterranean and North Africa, but she was the first to lose those opportunities. Before the outbreak of the Second World War there were talks about planning a major offensive against Egypt, with the aim of seizing Alexandria and the Suez Canal area, and also the possibility of linking-up with Italian East Africa via the Sudan. Had this been done, the Italians would have gained access to the Middle East and the Red Sea, as well as to the Indian Ocean, with all the possible consequences one can imagine. However, talks came to an end in 1939 when the Italian Navy, facing the threat of a joint Anglo-French menace in the event of war against both countries, openly stated the impossibility of supplying Libya. So the Western Desert turned into a secondary theatre of war, filled with second-rate troops only intended to hold out as long as possible in case of either a French or a British offensive.

The fall of France in June 1940, following shortly after Italy's declaration of war against her and Great Britain, brought no real change; with Britain apparently doomed by the German war machine, there was no urgent need for a major offensive against Egypt. Such a lack of strategic insight was matched by a lack of tactical and operational capabilities on the side of the Italian command in Libya. The Italian drive into Egypt, dictated by the political need to match the German offensive against Britain, was arranged using Kitchener's drive into Sudan in 1898 as an example with all its logistical preparation and slow, footslogged advance. The result was a nineteenth-century style offensive, which took no advantage of the available tanks shipped from Italy during the summer of 1940, and blunted the edge of Italian superiority in terms of men and materiel. The condition of Britain's forces at the time reveals the true extent of the missed opportunity; with the bulk of her army badly mauled at Dunkerque, Britain could only rely on the 7th Armoured Division (the other division in the area, 6th Infantry, was used to create the headquarters (HQ) of the Western Desert Force), and on those Imperial, Commonwealth and Dominion forces that became available. These included the 4th Indian Division plus, later on during the same year, the 6th Australian and the 2nd New Zealand divisions. As such, more than 220,000 Italians were faced by some 50,000 British and Commonwealth soldiers.

The First British Offensive: Operation Compass

The Italian advance to Sidi Barrani, started on 16 September 1940, soon turned from a potential threat against the British positions in Egypt into an opportunity. Churchill's decision to send a reinforcement of tanks to the area was not only bold, given the German threat against Britain, but was also an acknowledgement of how important the area was to the British strategy since, with the fall of France, this was the only land theatre of war left. The events that followed

BEDA FOMM

In February 1941 O'Connor's troops moved fast inland and across the desert, taking advantage of the Cyrenaica bulge (protruding north in the Mediterranean) to reach the coastal road at Beda Fomm, close to the narrow escape route to Tripoli. Surrounded, the Italian forces were quickly defeated on 7 February with the loss of 25,000 men.

would serve to reinforce how available means heavily influenced the war in the Western Desert. Directed by General Archibald Wavell, Commander-in-Chief in the Middle East, and led by General Richard O'Connor, Operation Compass was aimed at driving the Italians from the town of Sidi Barrani but, following their collapse, it turned into a major offensive that ended on 7 February 1941 at Beda Fomm after the Italian force had been destroyed. Total Italian losses for the Operation Compass were c.130,000, although figures are uncertain and probably include dead, wounded, POWs and the missing.

During the summer and autumn of 1940 Germany did actually consider the possibility of intervening in the Mediterranean, particularly because of the difficulties she faced with an invasion of the British Isles. Following the strategic thoughts of the German naval command, two basic aims were set: the seizure of both Gibraltar and the Suez Canal, which would have driven the Royal Navy out of the Mediterranean and given the Italians access to the Atlantic Ocean. Not only would the British positions in the Middle East have been in danger, but also the joint efforts of the German and Italian navies might have seriously endangered the sea lanes to Britain. Events soon turned these plans into nothing; both the German talks with the Spanish government about the attack against Gibraltar, and the Hitler–Mussolini talks about the deployment of a German Panzer Division in Libya, were inconclusive. Eventually, the ill-fated Italian attack against Greece, launched on 28 October, saw every strategic opportunity crumble.

By December 1940 the German Navy concluded that it was no longer possible to seek a strategic victory in the Mediterranean and, less than two months later, Hitler decided to send the Panzer Division to Libya, but only to prevent an Italian collapse.

Rommel Arrives

In February 1941, when the first German units arrived in Libya, it was Churchill's turn to re-direct Britain's strategic priorities; with the impending German attack against Greece, the decision was made to send British and Commonwealth forces to help defend the country. Since these could not come from anywhere other than the Middle East, that also meant the end of any chance to advance to Tripoli, regardless of whether this was actually possible. However, after only a few weeks the strategic settings were altered again: Italy sent the bulk of her mobile forces (the armoured 'Ariete' and the motorised 'Trento' and 'Trieste' divisions) to Libya, while Hitler decided to send

an entire Panzer corps – the future Afrika Korps. In the meantime one out of the three British and Commonwealth divisions in the Western Desert had been sent to Greece; the balance of power had turned again to the Axis' favour. The offensive started the following April by the commander of the Afrika Korps, the then

2. Field Marshal Erwin Rommel along with the Italian Governor of Libya, General Bastico.

rather unknown General Erwin Rommel, made things worse; still understrength, the Axis forces recaptured Cyrenaica and pushed on to the Libyan–Egyptian frontier, bypassing the crucial fortress of Tobruk, firmly held by the Australians.

Rommel's command significantly turned the war in the Western Desert into a matter of personalities; had he chosen to abide by his orders, things might have been different. But in the spring and summer of 1941 events were to unfold rapidly. While Rommel re-conquered Cyrenaica, in April the bulk of the Italian forces in East Africa surrendered, while in the Balkans the German offensive led to the seizure of both Yugoslavia and Greece, followed in May by the airborne capture of Crete. Also in May the uprising in Iraq was crushed by the British forces, who by mid-July also seized the Vichy (i.e. pro-German) forces in Syria. The German attack against the Soviet Union on 22 June 1941 turned, from the German point of view, the whole of the Mediterranean theatre into a sideshow. This was not true, however, for both Italy and Britain which, since then, focused their efforts on both the Western Desert and the Mediterranean, where a decisive battle was fought to keep the sea lanes open in order to reinforce and supply the Axis forces.

Means were again well short of the ends; Germany apart, both Britain and Italy (which, although busy on other fronts as well, had in the Mediterranean and the Western Desert their most active theatres of war) were still rebuilding their armies, which were largely spread serving duties in other areas (the Italians

CYRENAICA AND TOBRUK

Unlike Egypt, Cyrenaica (where the Western Desert campaign was fought until June 1942) is not entirely desert and is dominated, in the north, by the 'Green Mountains' massif. Its main harbour is Tobruk, 160km west of Egypt, which was the easternmost supply area for the Axis.

garrisoning the Balkans; the British in the Far East, in Africa, the Middle East and the Mediterranean, namely Gibraltar and Malta). Attention shifted to the Mediterranean, where the Royal Navy and the Royal Air Force (RAF) – mainly thanks to the possession of Malta – effectively succeeded in virtually cutting off the sea lanes to Libya by the end of 1941. Thanks also to the regrouping of the British and Commonwealth forces in the Western Desert, the new Middle East Commander, General Claude Auchinleck, launched on 18 November 1941 a major offensive (Operation Crusader) with the aim of relieving Tobruk. Worth noting is that, at the time, Britain provided about half of the forces for the operation, with the 7th Armoured and the 70th Infantry Division (built from the Western Desert Forces and used to replace the Australians at Tobruk), and the rest made up of the 1st South African, 2nd New Zealand and 4th Indian divisions. The newly formed British Eighth Army managed not only to relieve Tobruk, but also to inflict severe losses on Rommel's Panzer Army Africa, which on 8 December 1941 started a withdrawal west, back to their April starting positions.

Meanwhile developments in the Mediterranean, following the arrival of the German 2nd Air Fleet and of eighteen German submarines, undermined success on the battlefield; heavily attacked, the British sea and air forces were forced off from Malta, thus re-opening the sea lanes to Libya. Early in January 1942 Rommel received reinforcements, and on 21 January he attacked again, re-conquering western Cyrenaica up to the Gazala line, west of Tobruk.

From Tobruk to El Alamein

Once again, the strategic settings changed: the Japanese attack on Pearl Harbor brought the United States of America into the war, while in December 1941 the Soviet counterattack outside Moscow put an end to the German illusions of a swift victory on the Eastern Front. While forces were withdrawn from the Mediterranean, the Western Desert was to turn into one of the decisive theatres of war.

With both sides still understrength on the battlefield, the Germans and Italians reorganised their forces to the concept of 'more weapons, less men' (i.e. by having their units strongly armed but with less personnel); on the other side there were in May 1942 three British divisions, two of them armoured, alongside two South African and one Indian. The Axis leadership realised that control of the central Mediterranean, i.e. Malta, was vital to the war in the Western Desert since, given the role it played in strangling the Axis sea routes, only its neutralisation could re-open the supply lines. A plan was developed to seize Malta, and an agreement was reached with Rommel about its timing: he was to strike first in the desert, and after he managed to seize Tobruk the Italians and the Germans would attack Malta. Thus, having secured the sea lanes of supply, the Axis forces would have been able to plan a future offensive into Egypt.

Rommel's attack against the Gazala line, which was launched on 21 May 1942, soon turned into a major failure, with the bulk of the Afrika Korps trapped east of a large minefield and of the British defences. Poor command and leadership within the British Eighth Army, namely its commander General Neil Ritchie, overturned every possible advantage; uncoordinated British armoured attacks were repulsed by the German anti-tank guns, and eventually the Panzer Army Africa succeeded in crushing the British 150th Brigade. This allowed the Germans to open a passage through the minefields and to seize the southernmost position on the Gazala line, the Bir Hakeim stronghold, which had been held by a Free French brigade. Following the capture of another stronghold on the line on 13 June, British and Commonwealth forces withdrew east of Tobruk, which was attacked by Rommel on 20–21 June 1942. Defended again by Australian forces, this time the fortress could not withstand the attack as it had in 1941; the more experienced, and better prepared, Axis forces quickly seized Tobruk, also taking a huge booty in the process. This was the turning point in the Western Desert war; fully confident in his victory, and in the defeat of the enemy forces, Rommel managed to persuade the German

High Command that there was a chance to strike deep into Egypt, down to the Suez Canal. The plans to seize Malta (which apparently no-one had really believed in) were thus abandoned, and Rommel was given a green light for his offensive into Egypt.

Between June and July 1942 it did seem that the British positions in the Western Desert and the whole of the Middle East were threatened like never before. On 23 June the spearheads of the Afrika Korps crossed the Libyan–Egyptian border, while on the Eastern Front the Germans launched Operation Barbarossa and eventually reached Stalingrad and the Caucasus, leaving the Middle East open to attack. On 25 June the Panzer Army Africa attacked Mersa Matruh and seized it three days later, the Mediterranean Fleet vacated its base in Alexandria for Haifa. On 1 July the German and Italian forces attacked the Alamein line, and were soon to reveal how Auchinleck (who said Rommel's offensive 'was based on a bluff') had been right. Tired, and with its supply lines overstretched, the Panzer Army Africa's attack was called off two days later, and Rommel's army suffered its first, major crisis while facing the British and Commonwealth counterattacks that, starting on 10 July, would come to an end on the 28th with both sides digging a defensive line. Rommel's second attempt to break through the Alamein line started on 31 August–1 September 1942, eventually leading to the battle of Alam Halfa that was decided both by the stubborn British defence on the ridge and by the lack of supplies on the Axis side, namely the shortage of fuel.

As happens all too often, the twists of fate turned a would-be disaster into a major opportunity; Rommel's failure (and the failure of the German offensive on the Eastern Front) not only meant the Middle East was no longer in danger, but it also doomed the flawed Axis strategy in the Mediterranean and the Western Desert. In August Malta was reinforced, although still heavily under attack, the Axis sea lanes in the Mediterranean were threatened again and Alamein was no longer just a position to be held, but rather the place where the decisive battle of the Western Desert was to be fought. This was true for both sides: for the Axis, being forced

MALTA

Close to Sicily and on the route to Tripoli, the British-held island hosted naval and air bases from which the Royal Navy and the RAF successfully interdicted the sea lanes from Italy to Libya, impacting the enemy's ability to re-supply. However, the island was heavily attacked from the air, and suffered its own supply problems when the Axis beleaguered it.

out from Egypt would mean abandoning (publicly) every hope to reach Alexandria and the Suez Canal. For Britain, knowing that, in November, the American and British forces would have invaded the French colonies in North-West Africa, this was something like a last chance to defeat the enemy with her own forces.

The Opposing Forces

Both sides were reinforced, with the Italians throwing into the Western Desert the last of their best units (armoured and airborne), while, for the first time since July 1942, the size of the British Army forces surpassed those of its Commonwealth, Imperial and Dominion counterparts. With more than ten divisions or equivalents, six of them British and four from other countries (Australia, India, New Zealand and South Africa), the Eighth Army largely outnumbered its enemy with more than 220,000 men, approximately one thousand tanks and one thousand artillery pieces. On the contrary the Panzer Army Africa, which included four armoured (two German and two Italian) and two motorised divisions (one each), six infantry divisions (one German and five Italian, plus one German parachute brigade), only fielded some 110,000 men with about 500 tanks and 500 artillery pieces. Although enjoying some advantages, Rommel's forces now faced an Eighth Army onslaught that might not just simply dislodge the Axis forces from their positions, but rather completely destroy them.

Everyone knew what was at stake: if the Axis won, even if forced to withdraw back to Libya, there was still a chance to put Malta under pressure and re-open the sea lanes, thus prolonging the war in the Western Desert (or in North Africa) for many months, and making it very difficult for the Allies to invade Italy. On the other hand, if the British Eighth Army managed to defeat the Axis forces, or even to destroy them (as envisaged by Montgomery), the combined drive from both the east and the west would have brought to an end – after some twenty-six months of war – the presence of the Axis forces in the Western Desert and in North Africa as a whole, starting thus another phase in the war in the Mediterranean. For the first time since June 1940, at El Alamein, means and ends were finally equal.

3. Rommel's command staff posing in front of a captured AEC Matador armoured command vehicle; second from the right is Colonel Bayerlein, chief of staff of the Afrika Korps at El Alamein.

THE ARMIES

One of the peculiarities of the war in the Western Desert, hardly to be found in any other theatre of war, was how both sides were to take advantage of the booty taken from their adversaries. This ranged from simple clothing and uniform down to weapons (from the machine guns to the tanks), not to mention supplies – fuel for a start, but also food and water whenever possible. Indeed, sometimes it was quite hard to distinguish one side from the other, in many ways both armies were so similar.

The Commanders

Rommel's Early Supremacy

The Western Desert campaign was, more so than many others of the war, characterised by being largely dominated by modern mechanised warfare and, as such, was also heavily influenced by tactics, unit organisation, supplies and weaponry. However, one of the lessons of the 1940 campaign in the West was that no matter how superior an army may be in some or even all these fields, like the French Army was in many respects toward the Germans; still, superior command and leadership proved to be the decisive factors on the battlefield. This was particularly true during Operation Compass, when the stronger Italian Army was defeated

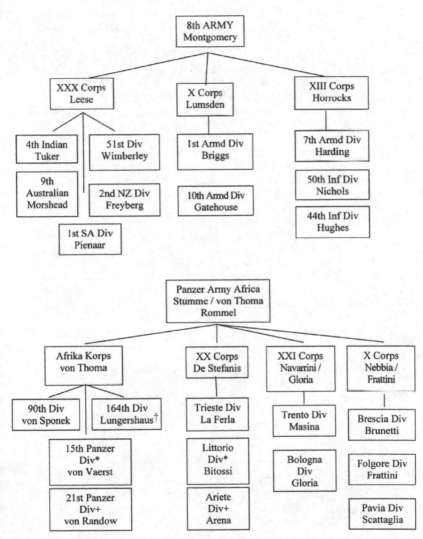

8th ARMY
Montgomery

XXX Corps
Leese

X Corps
Lumsden

XIII Corps
Horrocks

4th Indian
Tuker

51st Div
Wimberley

1st Armd Div
Briggs

7th Armd Div
Harding

9th
Australian
Morshead

2nd NZ Div
Freyberg

10th Armd Div
Gatehouse

50th Inf Div
Nichols

1st SA Div
Pienaar

44th Inf Div
Hughes

Panzer Army Africa
Stumme / von Thoma
Rommel

Afrika Korps
von Thoma

XX Corps
De Stefanis

XXI Corps
Navarrini /
Gloria

X Corps
Nebbia /
Frattini

90th Div
von Sponek

164th Div
Lungershaus†

Trieste Div
La Ferla

Trento Div
Masina

Brescia Div
Brunetti

15th Panzer
Div*
von Vaerst

Littorio
Div*
Bitossi

Bologna
Div
Gloria

Folgore Div
Frattini

21st Panzer
Div+
von Randow

Ariete
Div+
Arena

Pavia Div
Scattaglia

* Northern mobile group   + southern mobile group
† Full name – Lungershausen

Erwin Rommel

Born in 1891 near Ulm from a family with no military background, he was commissioned in 1910. During the First World War he distinguished himself on the battlefield, and, in 1917 he earned the highest award – the Pour le Mérite – for his role during the breakthrough of the Italian lines that led to the defeat at Caporetto. The fact that somebody else was at first given the award instead of him probably contributed to him in the future publicising his own successes as much as possible. A captain at the end of the war, he remained in the post-war army. Never a staff officer, his book 'Infantry Attacks' (1937) earned him fame and Hitler's attention. After commanding his headquarters, he was given command of the 7th Panzer Division, which he led successfully in France in 1940. Given command of the Afrika Korps on 3 February 1941 (he, like Montgomery, was a second choice too), and from 15 August of the newly formed Panzer Army Africa, the victory at Tobruk earned him the promotion to field marshal. Relentless, ambitious and energetic, Rommel became popular amongst his troops for his attitude to sharing their difficulties, but was often in trouble with both his subordinates and his superiors. Always a field commander but not a strategist, he was given command of Army Group B in France, and fought in Normandy in 1944 until he was wounded on 17 July. He committed suicide on 14 October because of his alleged involvement in the plot against Hitler.

4. Rommel aboard his half-tracked command vehicle, named 'Greif' (griffin).

by the Western Desert Force simply because its commander, Field Marshal Graziani, was not only a feeble leader but also still stuck to the nineteenth-century style of warfare, and was thus easily outmanoeuvred by the fast, mobile forces led by the British General Richard O'Connor, who managed to concentrate his forces against the Italian strongholds, taking them one by one.

There was a crucial factor in command and leadership during the Western Desert campaign, and that was the fact that practically none of the leaders stationed there actually possessed either an exact knowledge, or any kind of experience, with mechanised warfare in such an area. Experience gained during the first half of 1941 was therefore important, even more so than that gained during the last months while fighting in Operation Crusader. In this respect the Axis were, following the arrival of General Rommel, greatly advantaged over their adversaries for the very simple reason that Rommel soon turned into some kind of 'generalissimo', and was to lead both the German and the Italian units for most of the campaign, before sickness forced him to take leave in September 1942. Upon his arrival in Libya, Rommel was in fact subordinated tactically to the Italian theatre command, while also bound strategically to the German High Command's directives. Rommel's personality, part of his command and leadership qualities, soon brought him either to ignore orders or directives, or to bend them to suit his own needs, no matter where these actually came from.

ROMMEL'S REPLACEMENT

General Georg Stumme, who replaced Rommel at the head of the Panzer Army Africa up to his death on 24 October, fought in the Balkans and on the Eastern Front until June 1942, when he was found guilty of the loss of some restricted documents that had fallen into Soviet hands. Sentenced to five years, he was released thanks to his superiors and sent to Egypt.

This enabled him not only to become a sort of leading commander, which he actually was following the creation of the Panzer Army Africa (which practically put the Italian units under his command) in August 1941, but also to gain experience from his own mistakes.

Montgomery Takes Over

The opposite was true on the British side. Not only were commanders in the Western Desert subordinated to the Middle East Command, responsible for the entire theatre and its many needs as well, but also their frequent shifting meant that hardly any commanders could turn experience – including mistakes – into new lessons, and take advantage of them. In 1940–41 Middle East Command was held by General Archibald Wavell, with General Richard O'Connor in command of the Western Desert Force; Wavell was replaced shortly after O'Connor's capture during Rommel's drive into Cyrenaica in spring 1941 and, by the summer of 1941, there were both a new Middle East commander – General Claude Auchinleck – and a new Eighth Army commander, General Alan Cunningham. The latter's poor performances during Operation Crusader led to him being replaced right in the middle of the battle by General Neil Ritchie, who was himself eventually sacked after the Tobruk disaster in 1942. General Auchinleck took over command of the Eighth Army on 25 June.

Regardless of any possible evaluation of British generalship in the Western Desert, one ought to remark on the fact that Rommel was to face five different commanders on the field (not including Middle East Command) before General Bernard Law Montgomery was eventually appointed Eighth Army's commander in August 1942. Without comparing Auchinleck's and Montgomery's command and leadership qualities, it is undoubtedly true that the latter's strong-willed, simple and straightforward method of command would bring a rather necessary, not to say also welcome, change to an otherwise crippled situation, until then largely dominated by uncertainty, dispersion and infighting.

Bernard Law Montgomery

When he took over command of the Eighth Army, 'Monty' knew well he had two enemies: the Panzer Army Africa and its commander, Rommel.

Born 1887 in London, but of Anglo-Irish descent, as son of a bishop he was quite an outsider in the still socially restricted Army Officers Corps. After the Royal Military College at Sandhurst, he was commissioned in the Royal Warwickshire Regiment in 1908. His first four years of service were spent in India, and he was severely wounded shortly after the outbreak of the First World War in 1914. Awarded a DSO, he served then as a staff officer and, after the Staff College at Camberley, became a major in 1920 and was eventually promoted major general in 1938. In 1939 he was given command of 3rd Division, and he was to briefly command II Corps at Dunkerque. For the next two years he was in Britain with the Home Army, until he took over command of the Eighth Army as a second choice (General Gott, chosen for the command, died in an air crash). His self-confidence, coupled with an irksome personality, largely contributed to his unpopularity with subordinates and fellow commanders, even though his strict handling of discipline and training were amongst the factors that contributed to his military successes. Promoted general and knighted after Alamein, he became a field marshal on 1 September 1944 and was raised to peerage in 1946, when he became Chief of Imperial General Staff. Retired in 1958, he died at his home near Alton, Hampshire, in 1976.

5. *General Montgomery, wearing the Australian bush hat, standing atop a Crusader tank.*

Also, Montgomery's lack of innovative or broadsighted views, coupled with his lack of experience with Western Desert warfare, would come at the right moment for Alamein was, for the first time since the war had started in this theatre, an area not really suitable for mobile, mechanised warfare, especially given the conditions of the two opposing armies. This eventually led 'Monty' to beat Rommel using a very simple command method: sticking to what he knew his forces could do without even trying to face the 'Desert Fox' on his terms, which many other British commanders had mistakenly tried to do.

The Soldiers

The Allied Forces

One of the reasons behind the success of O'Connor's offensive of 1940–41 was the availability of some of the finest men and units in the British Army. The 7th Armoured Division (famously nicknamed the 'Desert Rats') had been formed in fact from the Mobile Force, itself created by General Percy Hobart, one of the leading innovative minds of the interwar period. Formed by a small group of pre-war regular, professional soldiers, the Western Desert Force also relied on the contribution of the 4th Indian Division first, and of the 6th Australian in the second part of the offensive.

The role played by the Commonwealth, Imperial and Dominion forces can hardly be underestimated for, until the summer of 1942, they provided about the half of the combat units that faced the Panzer Army Africa. Being reorganised after Dunkerque, the British Army would in fact mostly provide armoured units, those most suited for the battlefeld, while the others were mainly infantry formations. It ought to be said that they actually excelled in that role, demonstrated by the excellent performances of the Australian infantry during the early phases of the siege at Tobruk in April–May 1941.

In 1939 the Australian Army only comprised a very small number of regulars, less than 3,000, out of an army numbering some

83,000. Given the reluctance of the Australian government to impose sacrifices again to a population already suffering from the losses of the First World War, the four divisions eventually raised for overseas service (6th, 7th, 8th and 9th) were made exclusively of volunteers, while conscription was introduced only for service in the home defence force. In June 1940 the 1st Australian Corps (with 6th, 7th and 9th divisions) were deployed in the Middle East and, from February 1941, part of the 6th Division joined British and New Zealand forces in Greece, eventually fighting alongside them at Crete the following May.

The Australian forces were to suffer most from the constant shifting of units to and from the front; while the 9th Australian Division held the Tobruk fortress (relieved in October by the rebuilt British 70th Infantry Division), the 7th Australian Division fought in Syria before being eventually withdrawn, along with the 6th Division early in 1942. The 9th Division only returned to the front in July 1942, and was actually withdrawn back to Australia after the Alamein battle.

Losses suffered by the Australian Army in the war against Germany totalled 19,351 troops, which included 3,552 killed (2,610 of which in action), 6,874 prisoners and 8,925 wounded or injured, clearly demonstrating the true extent of its involvement in the Western Desert war.

A similar fate was to befall other non-British forces. The Indian Army, which in 1939 was an all-volunteer force, still largely led by

HOBART'S 'FUNNIES'

General Sir Percy Hobart formed the 7th Armoured Division in Egypt, but retired in 1939. Rescued from retirement by Churchill in 1941, he first formed the 11th and then the 79th Armoured Division, the latter equipped with special Royal Engineers armoured vehicles (nicknamed 'Hobart's funnies'), used to open passages across minefields and other obstacles.

British officers, rose from an initial strength of 352,000 in 1939 (comprising 205,000 Indians), to a total strength of 2,500,000 by the end of the war, making it the largest all-volunteer army. India's relative proximity to the Middle East, coupled with the ongoing reorganisation of the British Army, led to the early deployment of the 4th Indian Division in Egypt, which in December 1940 was to take part in O'Connor's offensive, before being relieved by the 6th Australian Division. The 4th Indians were transferred to the frontline again in November 1941 and were deployed during Operation Crusader, but were replaced by the 5th Indians (who had fought the Italians in East Africa), plus elements of the 10th Indian Division, in May 1942 at Gazala. However, the 4th Indian Division was ordered back to the frontline in June–July 1942, while the 5th was withdrawn to Burma. Meanwhile, 4th, 8th and 10th Indian divisions fought until 1945, eventually taking part in the Italian campaign.

Unlike the Indian Army, the South African Army was only a small contingent that in September 1939 totalled just 5,385 men. Recruited on a voluntary basis too, although black soldiers were excluded from combat duties, the South Africans eventually formed three infantry divisions and first saw action in East Africa before being redeployed to Egypt, just in time to take part in Operation Crusader. By September 1941 there were some 60,000 (plus some other 15,000 black) South African soldiers in Egypt, in fact the peak of South Africa's war effort. Not a lucky one, since Crusader was the first of a series of unfortunate engagements which saw the South African forces suffering heavy losses; during the battle of Sidi Rezegh the 1st South African Division lost one-third of its strength, while the 2nd Division lost more than 10,722 at Tobruk in June 1942, being practically wiped out. Like the Australian 9th Division, the 1st South Africans were withdrawn after Alamein, eventually to be used to create the 6th Armoured Division that fought in Italy from April 1944.

Last, but not least, New Zealand's contribution to the Western Desert campaign was to turn into quite an important one; with a population of only 1,630,000, New Zealanders were to suffer more losses than any other part of the British Empire. The 2nd New Zealand Expeditionary Force (NZEF), as opposed to the 1st NZEF in the First World War, eventually represented the equivalent of twenty-five British divisions in proportion to the population. The first echelons of the New Zealand Division (officially redesignated 2nd New Zealand Division in June 1942) arrived in Egypt in February 1940, and until March 1941 the division was scattered between the Middle East and the United Kingdom. Subsequently, it fought in Greece and at Crete, taking part in the relief of Tobruk during Operation Crusader in November 1941. This first period saw the loss of some 10,000 men, which was followed by further severe losses in June and July 1942, when the division was deployed in the battles at Mersa Matruh and the first at Alamein – its total strength shrinking from 20,000 to 13,000 in a single month. Called the spearhead of the Eighth Army, the 2nd New Zealand Division should have been withdrawn after Alamein, but it eventually fought all the way until the end of the war in Italy.

One of the greatest problems the Eighth Army faced during the Western Desert campaign was the constant shifting of its forces, all too often redeployed elsewhere for other duties or simply withdrawn from the frontline, with the consequence of an ever-changing order of battle. With some twenty divisions under command in 1941–42, it is quite remarkable that no more than four to five of them actually fought in more than two battles for a prolonged period of time. Such a state of affairs led on the one hand to the eventual rest and refit of some divisions, which would be returned to the front fully restored; on the other hand, this prevented those units from gaining – and making a good use – of the same experience and hardship that characterised the German and elite Italian forces.

These problems were particularly true for the British Army which, apart from the units previously mentioned, was (since September 1939) a conscript force. Whatever advantage this may have been in terms of manpower availability, this was to be largely wasted because of a series of factors. Firstly, men (either volunteers or drafted) were allowed to choose a branch of service, which meant that the keener ones, and often best fitted, chose either the Royal Navy or the Royal Air Force. The creation of a large number of special forces, such as the Commandos, also drained and eventually dispersed a large number of the men more suitable for combat. Furthermore, infantry was no longer seen as the queen of the battlefield and, by October 1941, only three out of ten soldiers were serving in it. Armoured units were not the only ones to receive a large intake, for the proportion of 'tooth to tail' (the ratio between combat (tooth) and service, supply and support (tail) troops) also increased to the latter's favour and, at the same time, about a quarter of the men in the army belonged to supplies, services and technical units.

All these factors largely contributed to a widespread dispersion of the army units and the divisions in particular, only a portion of which would actually see action on the battlefield (nine out of the eleven armoured divisions formed, twenty-five out of a total of thirty-four infantry divisions formed). The developments of the Western Desert Force, or the Eighth Army from 26 September 1941, are meaningful; in April 1941 the inexperienced and understrength 2nd Armoured Division, that had been sent to the Middle East in October 1940, was destroyed during Rommel's first offensive into Cyrenaica. The lack of experienced units was clear by November 1941, when Operation Crusader started and the Eighth Army only deployed two British divisions on the frontline: the experienced 7th Armoured Division and the 70th Infantry Division, which was the rebuilt (and renumbered) 6th Division reformed from the Western Desert Force. The fact that, after Crusader, this was sent to the Far East and eventually split up to form special forces units is a clear waste of the experience those men had gained.

By the time of the Gazala battle in May 1942, the situation had barely improved since the British Army had at the front only two armoured (1st and 7th) and one infantry divisions (50th, first time in action since the redeployment to the Middle East in April 1941),

The Eighth Army Soldier

In October 1942 the Eighth Army was a mixture of all kind of troops, only partially accustomed to the desert either because many were newly arrived replacements, or fresh units transferred from Britain. It did not take long before personal experience, or the valuable lessons given by veterans, quickly led to adaptation in a whole variety of matters. Dress turned from formal to practical, with large use of desert boots and shorts during the day along with the useful scarf and sand goggles, the only protection actually available. Sand was in fact everybody's nightmare for it was everywhere, not just around the soldiers but also on their clothes, and above all in their food. Availability of large quantities of canned food, particularly canned beef, made Eighth Army soldiers' diet satisfactory, although not always palatable. Water was a sore subject, with all too often less than five litres per man per day, inclusive of cooking, washing and drinking which, generally, was limited to a single litre per day. The basic rule of 'if in doubt, brew it' was also a necessity, since tea was more drinkable than water. Regardless of lack of water, personal hygiene was more than just a commodity in the desert; hot weather and sand would turn any scratch, cut or graze into an infected 'desert sore' spreading all over the body. In such conditions, even small comforts like adequate shelters, some 'V' cigarettes and Stella beer were much appreciated, though not as much as leave to Alexandria or Cairo.

6. *Eighth Army's infantry advancing First World War style, with bayonets fixed.*

plus another three armoured and one motor infantry brigade. The fact that the 10th Armoured Division, which had been formed in August 1941 from the 1st Cavalry Division deployed in the Middle East early in 1940, only saw first action in June–July 1942 is revealing of the delay with which the British Army was able to face the needs of the Western Desert war.

In fact, it was only after the summer of 1942 that the British Army committed a large number of its units to this area and it is well worth noting how those units – which included the 1st, 7th and 10th Armoured, 44th, 50th and 51st Infantry divisions – were eventually to form its backbone during the campaigns that followed in Tunisia, Italy, Normandy and North-West Europe.

The Axis Forces

The Italian Army was made exclusively of draftees, and since, from an Italian strategic perspective, Libya and Italian East Africa would be lost in the event of war against France and Great Britain, the area was filled with second-rate infantry units only intended to hold the colony as long as possible. Few changes took place after the fall of France, and while the actual army organisation remained the same – with its two field armies (Fifth and Tenth), and twelve infantry or equivalent divisions ('Pavia', 'Bologna', 'Brescia', 'Savona', 'Sabratha', 'Sirte', 'Marmarica', 'Catanzaro', 'Cirene' and three Blackshirts divisions), plus two Libyan divisions – one ad hoc armoured brigade ('Babini', after its commander) was formed using two medium tank battalions shipped from Italy. The destruction of the Tenth Army at Sidi Barrani and Beda Fomm also meant the annihilation of seven infantry divisions and of the two Libyan divisions, leaving only some four operational divisions (Pavia, Bologna, Brescia and Savona, all lacking artillery), plus the badly mauled Sabratha. The belated acknowledgement of the Western Desert as a 'mechanised' theatre of war, along with the readdressing of the Italian strategic priorities, meant that new units sent to Libya were either armoured or motorised; these included,

7. *Italian medium tanks of the Ariete Division.*

between January and September 1941, the armoured Ariete, and the motorised Trento and Trieste divisions. Although far from being the real elite, a status both the Ariete and the Trieste would earn on the battlefield, they still were the bulk of the Italian strategic reserve and, given their actual equipment, had been better trained than the rest of the army.

The Italian forces in the Western Desert formed thus two different armies: one army made of mobile, mechanised units roughly comparable to the German Afrika Korps – the Ariete and the Trieste, forming the mobile army corps (later renamed XX Army Corps) – and the other one made of footslogged infantry, used initially to lay siege around Tobruk and, in 1942, to hold the line and deliver feint attacks against the Gazala line. Manpower and organisation were only one of the many problems afflicting the

Italian Army in Libya; lack of motor vehicles meant that losses could hardly be replaced, and so the Trento Division was downgraded to an infantry one in autumn 1941. On the other hand, infantry were well down the requirements list with the consequence that, between June 1940 and October 1942 only some 195,000 men were sent to North Africa (which was about one-fourth of the total strength sent to Albania). Taking into account the fact that the Italians also had to secure Libya and the Sahara, losses and attrition meant that, by early 1942, frontline units lacked strength and a major reorganisation was needed; this led to the new 'type 1942' divisional organisation based on the 'less men, more weapons' concept which the Germans developed at the same time. However, on the Italian side that actually meant that infantry divisions were to shrink to a total strength of less than 7,000, and even the Ariete and the Trieste were to have an established strength of 8,300 and 6,700. In fact, actual strength was always much lower than the established strength: between May and June 1942 both the Bologna and Brescia divisions only had an average of some 4,500 men, while both Pavia and Sabratha's strengths fell down from some 4,400 to about 3,000. The Trento Division did maintain a strength of some 5,000, while that of the Trieste dropped from 6,700 to 4,700, and the Ariete actually increased from 6,800 to 7,200. Considering that by mid-1942 most of the Italian soldiers in Libya had not had any period of leave back home,

'MORE WEAPONS, LESS MEN'

After the heavy losses suffered during Operation Crusader, the Axis forces in the Western Desert were reorganised by reducing personnel in their establishments, given the scarcity of replacements. In the meantime, units were allotted more and heavier weapons, which led to the 'more weapons, less men' concept.

it is hardly surprising that the Italians were to gravely suffer from a manpower crisis during the first Alamein battle.

In July the Sabratha (now some 2,000 strong) was annihilated by an Australian attack and subsequently disbanded, while the badly mauled Pavia was downgraded as fit for rear area duties only. Like the Germans, the Italians brought reinforcements to Egypt as well; these included the 'Littorio' Armoured Division, which since the spring had been deployed at Tripoli ready to seize Tunisia in case of need (needless to say, this was a task the division was not able to perform when actually required to do so), and the 'Folgore' Parachute Division, which had been formed to be part of the assault force against Malta. At the time of the second Alamein battle, the Italians had a nucleus of experienced and battle-worthy divisions like the Ariete and the Trieste, one single real elite unit like the Folgore Division and a large number of understrength infantry divisions, able only (at the best) to hold the line.

The Italian debacle of winter 1940–41 made the German intervention in Libya necessary, at first with the simple aim of delivering a 'blocking force' to halt the British advance. The first German unit sent to Libya in February 1941 was the 5th Light Division, in fact an ad hoc unit built around the bulk of 3rd Panzer Division's armoured units (this was the unit that in 1940 should have been sent to Libya) and a rather large amount of anti-tank and anti-aircraft units. Hitler's decision to create the Afrika Korps

INFANTRY IN THE DESERT

Often referred to as a mobile and mechanised war, the campaign in the Western Desert also included a great deal of footslogged infantry – soldiers lacking any form of motor transport. Most of the Italian infantry units did not have their own vehicles, and soldiers were required to march on foot unless these could be provided.

was followed by the decision to send to Libya the newly formed 15th Panzer Division as well, although its actual arrival in the area was delayed and it could not help to prevent the Australians from holding the Tobruk fortress. In August 1941, shortly before the creation of Panzer Army Africa Command, both divisions were reorganised, and the 5th Light was renamed 21st Panzer Division: their established strength stood at about 13–14,000, although it was actually lower. Facing a shortage of infantry, the reorganisation had actually seen 21st Panzer Division reinforced with some of 15th Panzer Division's infantry units, already in late June, and those of the 90th Light 'Africa' Division, with both newly arrived units and others already available on the spot; in fact, at the time of the Gazala battle it was still forming and it was not until August 1942, after the reorganisation undertaken in early 1942, that it reached its peak established strength of some 14,500. Both 15th and 21st Panzer divisions were also reorganised on the 'more weapons, less men' concept, their actual strength dropping to some 11,000.

Like the Italian Army, the German units were to suffer from attrition too; the fast advance into Egypt, and the battles fought at Matruh and Alamein, depleted a rather small force and, in July, Rommel was to face a crisis in the Afrika Korps too. Replacements and reinforcements were brought in, this time focusing on infantry; in July and August both the Parachute Brigade 'Ramcke' (named after its commander, intended to attack Malta like the Folgore Division) and the 164th Light 'Africa' Division, formed from units deployed at Crete, were sent to Egypt to add some 18,000 men to the Panzer Army Africa strength. However, their hurried redeployment, right in the middle of the desert in full summer, made any kind of acclimatisation impossible. The consequence was that while the Germans reached their peak strength in the desert, they also suffered from a similar increase in sicknesses. To this was added the poor overall quality of some of the replacements, which eventually led Rommel to notice how, at the time of Montgomery's offensive at El Alamein, the Panzer

The Panzer Army Africa Soldier

Largely unaccustomed to tropics and the desert, the Germans faced many troubles from their arrival in Libya. Their situation actually worsened in Egypt, mainly because the overstretched supply lines and the priority given to fuel and ammunition soon led to a widespread lack of food and water. During the summer of 1942 both German and Italian soldiers experienced hunger for the first time since the beginning of the Western Desert campaign. Only from late September–early October did the situation improve, but a heavy toll had already been paid. During the last months of the campaign the Panzer Army had an average of more than 10,000 cases of sickness, mostly due to the hot weather and the inadequate diet (water too was scarcely available, and the daily ration to drink was limited to a single canteen per soldier, which is three quarters of a litre). Lack of most of the commodities and the comforts largely available to Eighth Army soldiers, at least that was the general perception, further aggravated the miserable life of the German and Italian soldier, who considered any kind of canned food, drink or liquor captured from the enemy an enviable booty! Additionally, unlike the Eighth Army, most of the Axis veterans in the desert had no chance at all to enjoy anything like leave to Cairo, and could only partly comfort themselves with the popular tune 'Lili Marlene', which was aired every night on the radio.

8. German soldiers in the desert. Second El Alamein was the first infantry battle to be fought in the Western Desert and in North Africa.

Army seriously suffered from a shortage of personnel; not only did it lack some 17,000 men, but of those available no more than a third were desert veterans, or the kind of soldiers Rommel was used to relying on.

The Kit

The Allies

One of the characteristics of the soldiers in the British, Australian, Indian, South African and New Zealand armies that fought in the Western Desert campaign was that, regardless of their nationality and the unit they belonged to, their appearance was practically always the same, with the most notable exceptions of the headgear used by the Australian and New Zealand, not to mention the Indian, soldiers.

However, in spite of first appearances, there were peculiar differences in their uniforms and equipment: a noticeable difference was the steel helmet used by the Australians which, in spite of a remarkable similarity to the British Mark II helmet, was in fact home produced. At their arrival in the Middle East soldiers were given a sort of 'tropical kit', which included a tropical pith helmet, a khaki drill shirt and shorts, long woollen socks and woollen hose tops, cloth puttees or gaiters, leather ankle boots (ammunition boots), and a woollen cardigan, while retaining the European uniform made of battledress blouse and trousers, and the greatcoat. A khaki drill service dress was also issued, made of an open collar jacket with four pockets and long trousers. The cardigan, like the European battledress and greatcoat, was used as protection from the cold at night, and items such as leather jerkins and sheepskin coats were also used during the winter in temperate areas like northern Cyrenaica. Pith helmets were replaced in battle by the steel helmet, and during service by forage caps, berets (mainly tank and armoured units), bonnets (Scottish units), and the usual Australian bush hat and the Indian turban when necessary.

The 1937 pattern web equipment was used in the Mediterranean
and Europe as well; it was made of canvas with a large belt to
which two universal web pouches were fitted (these could carry
magazines for the Bren gun, as well as ammunition clips for the
rifle and hand grenades), with two braces worn over the shoulders,
crossing at the back and buckled to the rear of the belt. A bayonet
'frog' (a leather or canvas sheath) and canteen, both secured to the
web, were usually worn along – since 1942 – with an entrenching
tool made of a spade and separate handle; packs (either small
or large) were also used to carry other items, as well as the anti-
gas equipment, never popular and seldom used. Officers had the
customary pistol holster and ammo pouch. The most common
weapons did not differ much from those used during the First
World War, these were the Webley .38 revolver, the Mark III Short
Magazine Lee Enfield .303 rifle, and the US Thompson M1928 .45
sub-machine gun; heavy weapons included the .303 Bren light

9. *Two 'Tommies' manning a 2in. mortar wearing the full kit, including
backpacks and entrenching tools.*

COMFORTABLE OR NOT?

Two items of tropical clothing became famous, for different reasons. The Italian 'sahariana' jacket was well cut and could be easily worn with or without a shirt which, along with the good cotton used, made it popular. British 'Bombay bloomers' – trousers, cut to be folded into shorts, were too large and unpractical, which made them unpopular.

machine gun (with a 29 round magazine, which could fire 500 rounds per minute), the .303 Vickers Mark I heavy machine gun (firing 400–500 rounds per minute), 2in. and 3in. mortars and the .55 Boys Mark I anti-tank rifle that could penetrate some 14mm of armour at 500 metres. The No. 36 Mills hand grenade, with different weights, was standard. The gap between the light Bren gun and the heavy Vickers made both German and Italian machine guns, whenever available, much appreciated; on 23 October the 9th Australian Division had seventy-one German machine guns, twenty-eight light and nine heavy Italian machine guns.

The Axis

The Italian tropical uniform was slightly different from the British version; made of khaki cotton, it was cut in a way similar to the grey-green European uniform (also used in winter and temperate areas) with an open collar jacket and four pockets, a shirt, breeches worn with cloth puttees, and ankle boots. Unlike the British, the Italians liked their tropical pith helmet and wore them for almost every occasion, often preferring them to the model 1933 steel helmet. A much welcome addition in 1942 was a peaked field cap, similar to the German version. The most interesting, and widely appreciated, item of Italian uniform was the 'sahariana' jacket, with its typical 'winged' chest pockets; very comfortable in every condition, it was used by officers and a variant (a blouse) was also produced for the other ranks. Folgore Division paratroopers wore the special forces' collarless version of the sahariana, although at Alamein they were seen mostly barebacked wearing only shorts and the pith helmet (paratroopers were issued with rubber-soled jump boots, a unique rarity in the Italian Army, but these had to be replaced with standard boots while in Egypt because the rubber melted). Italians greatly appreciated, like the Germans, items captured from the British and in particular the shorts, which were longer and more comfortable than their (and the German) version.

Personal equipment was quite different; soldiers only had a small brown leather belt, with an inverted 'U' shaped loop running around the neck to support two magazine pouches worn on the front. The belt was also used to carry the bayonet frog, but both the canteen and the canvas gas mask canister, or alternatively a breadbag (a small haversack), were worn with their own straps. Officers used a leather 'Sam Browne' style belt and sling, which ran across the chest, over the right shoulder and carried the pistol holster. Weapons included the semi-automatic 9mm Beretta 34 pistol (which, according to a popular joke, was more lethal if thrown at the enemy), as well as different versions of the 6.5mm Mannlicher-Carcano 91 muskets, the most typical one with a foldable bayonet. The 6.5mm Breda 30 light machine gun was the equivalent of the Bren with a 20 cartridge magazine and a rate of 400–500 rounds per minute, although it lacked reliability, while the 8mm Breda 37 and Fiat 35 heavy machine guns (with a rate of fire of 450 rounds per minute) were preferable to the Vickers, being air cooled. Paratroopers only were issued the Beretta 38 9mm sub-machine gun. Additionally, 2in. and 3in. mortars were available, along with different types of anti-tank rifles. Italian hand grenades were too light and scarcely effective.

The Germans were latecomers to tropical warfare, and heavily relied on their First World War experience; in 1940–41 a tropical uniform was issued, made of olive-coloured cotton with an open collar field blouse with four pockets, a cotton shirt, long and short trousers (too short and not very popular, unless at rest), lace-up canvas and leather boots, either knee or ankle length (the latter being preferred), and a greatcoat. Pith helmets were issued and used for a while, replaced by the standard Model 35 steel helmet in combat, but both the standard forage cap and the newly issued field peaked cap were much more popular. A canvas waist belt and 'Y' shaped suspenders were made to match their European equivalent; cartridge pouches were two groups of three (leather), and normal equipment worn on the belt included an entrenching tool, bayonet frog, breadbag and canteen, while on the back an 'assault' kit could be worn to carry a tent quarter and a mess kit. The characteristic metal, round gas mask canister was worn with its own straps. In the field, these uniforms proved uncomfortable and scarcely resistant, and whenever possible either Italian or British items were used.

Standard weapons in use included the 9mm semi-automatic Walther P38 or Luger P08, the 7.92mm Mauser carbine 98K, and the 9mm MP38/40 machine pistol (the 'Schmeisser'), a reliable and much appreciated weapon. The Germans did not have light or heavy machine guns, but rather a single, standard machine gun which was used either as a light machine gun when firing from its

10. German infantry marching in the desert, all well laden. The man on the left is carrying a MG34 light machine gun.

own bipod, or as a heavy machine gun if mounted on its foldable tripod mount. The standard machine gun was the 'Spandau' or 7.92mm MG34 that could fire 800–900 rounds per minute. This already very effective weapon was matched by the new version, the MG42, some samples of which were also used at Alamein; similar in its design, this could fire 900–1,200 rounds per minute, making it one of the most lethal weapons used in the Western Desert. On the other hand, the 7.92mm PzB38 and 39 anti-tank rifles were not quite as effective, while both the 50mm and 81mm mortars were. The German hand grenades were quite different from all others, with their characteristic stick and rounded cap, 36cm long, these were very effective too since the stick enabled soldiers to throw them over longer distances, and their explosive charge made them lethal in a 20-metre radius.

While no great improvement was seen in infantry weapons, tanks and anti-tank guns were constantly improved during the whole Western Desert campaign. In 1940 the Italian Army was quite behind in tank development, in spite of producing relatively large numbers; in 1940 about half of its tank strength in Libya was made of the light L3 tankette, weighing 3 tons and armed with twin 8mm machine guns in the hull. The rest was made of the medium M11 tank (100 produced), 11 tons of weight armed with a 37mm gun in the hull and two 8mm machine guns in the turret, and of the newly produced M13/40 tanks, weighing 14 tons, with a frontal armour of 30mm, armed with a 47mm gun in the turret and two 8mm machine guns in the hull. British tanks were roughly equivalent with the light Mark VI (5.2 tons, armed with a twin Vickers machine guns in the turret), and the Marks I, II and IV Cruiser tank (13–14 tons, one 2 pounder gun and two to three Vickers or Besa machine guns, armour 14–30mm). The arrival of the Matilda II Infantry Tanks, which equipped 7th Royal Tank Regiment during O'Connor's offensive, was to make the difference; this 27-ton tank with a frontal armour of 78mm, though still armed with a 2 pounder gun and one machine gun, was virtually invulnerable to the Italian tanks and anti-tank guns,

11. A Universal Carrier and a Matilda infantry tank; early British victories against the Italians in 1940–41 came thanks to this tank, practically invulnerable to Axis anti-tank guns.

the latter being the 47/32 gun which was roughly equivalent to the British standard 2 pounder (40mm) gun. Actually, the latter could penetrate up to 40mm of armour at 1,000 metres, a performance which the Italian gun could only achieve at some 500 metres.

The German tanks brought some innovations to the armoured warfare in the Western Desert, though they were hardly superior to their British equivalent. Apart from the light Panzer II tank (9 tons, armed with a 20mm gun and a 7.92mm machine gun in the turret), used along with the few Panzer I tanks in a reconnaissance role (the latter roughly the equivalent of the Italian L3 tankette, 21st Panzer Division had twenty of them in August 1941), the bulk of German armour was provided by the medium Panzer III tank, which in its version 'G' weighed 20 tons, had a 50mm gun, two 7.92mm machine guns and a frontal armour of 30mm, and was the standard main battle tank. The medium Panzer IV (weight 20–21 tons, armed with a short-barrelled 75mm gun and two 7.92mm machine guns, armour 30mm thick in the 'D' and 'E' versions) was intended to provide support, although it was also used against enemy tanks. Even the Italian tanks saw some improvements, although the

Ariete Division arrived in Libya still equipped with some 120 light L3 tankettes (twenty-four of them armed with a flamethrower), by the autumn of 1941 it had been re-equipped with both the M13/40 and the new M14/41 tanks, the latter an improved version with a more powerful engine and slightly thicker (42mm) frontal armour. The British tank inventory also saw some changes; the light Mark VI was soon withdrawn, followed in late 1941 – mostly after Operation Crusader – by the Mark I, II and IV Cruiser tanks, and the Mark II Matilda. Early the same year the new Mark VI Crusader tank was introduced, weighing 20 tons, armed with a 6 pounder (57mm) gun and one or two Besa 7.92mm machine guns, and with a frontal armour 51mm thick. This was followed in July 1941 by the American-built M3 'Stuart' or 'Honey' tank as the British tank crews renamed it (thanks to its reliability and handling) which, although a light tank weighing 12 tons, was armed with a 37mm gun and two

12. A German Panzer IV tank blown up from the inside.

.30 or .50 machine guns, and had a frontal armour up to 57mm thick. Later on the Mark III Valentine was introduced; an infantry tank weighing 16 tons and armed with a 2 pounder gun (6 pounder since spring 1942), and with frontal armour 65mm thick.

As a matter of fact, the German (not to mention the Italian) armour did not enjoy any kind of superiority against their British adversaries, rather the opposite in many cases since the 6 pounder gun was able to penetrate their armour even at more than 1,000-metre range. On the contrary, the German 50mm gun could only penetrate some 36–42mm (the latter only when using the improved, tungsten-core, armour piercing grenade) at the same range. German armour could only effectively deal with the more heavily armoured British tanks at a range of 100 metres using the short-barrelled 75mm gun of the Panzer IV tank. Even the German anti-tank guns available, the 37mm 35/36 and the new 50mm 38 guns, were scarcely effective; the former, only able to penetrate some 29mm thick armour at 500 metres, was virtually useless and was therefore nicknamed 'door knocker'. The latter, able to penetrate 59–72mm at 500 metres, was quite a good weapon though mainly useful at close range. Only the dual purpose anti-tank and anti-aircraft 88mm gun, able to penetrate more than 120mm armour at 2,000 metres, was a real tank killer, but it was available in very limited quantities and only thirty-nine of them were at the front in August 1942. The Germans were, on the other hand, the first to recognise the need for an improved anti-tank capability, and reacted promptly even if mostly with impromptu solutions; using the Soviet-built 76.2mm gun, large quantities of which had been captured during the early stages of the attack against the Soviet Union, they managed to provide a suitable anti-tank gun able to deal with the British tanks. Available either as a towed gun or on a self-propelled mount (either on the chassis of the Czech-built Panzer 38 tank, or on that of the German 7-ton prime mover), it could penetrate 82–94mm thick armour at 1,000 metres, being still very effective at a 1,500-metre range (up to 2,000 metres).

13. A German 88mm dual purpose gun in action, still mounted on its wheeled carriage.

14. Loading ammunition into an M3 Lee/Grant tank.

It was in fact thanks to this 'tank buster' that Rommel's Afrika Korps was able to deal with the British armour during the Gazala battle in May–June 1942. At the time, the latter had seen a major improvement thanks to the arrival of the American-built M3 medium Lee/Grant tank, weighing 29 tons, armed with a hull mounted 75mm gun and a turret mounted 37mm gun (plus one to three .30–.50 machine guns), and with a frontal armour 57mm thick. First met at Gazala, it came as an immense shock to the Germans who managed to deal with it mainly thanks to their 76.2mm guns. In the meantime, new Axis armour became available; the Italians introduced their 75mm self-propelled gun (15 tons, 50mm thick armour), along with the first samples of the German long-barrelled 50mm and 75mm guns, Panzer III 'J' and Panzer IV 'F' arrived and, thanks to their improved guns (the former could penetrate 57–72mm of armour at 500 metres, the latter 72mm at 1,500 metres) and armour (50mm thick), gained an edge over their adversaries.

Thanks to the arrival of the American-built M4 medium Sherman tank (50 tons, 75mm main gun and two machine guns, 76mm thick armour), along with the 6 pounder anti-tank gun, the British Army regained that edge in time for the Alamein

MONTY'S 'SECRET WEAPON'

The American-built M4 medium Sherman tank was Montgomery's 'secret weapon' at El Alamein. With good armour and a top speed of some 30km per hour on rugged terrain, it was armed with a 75mm M3 gun which could fire and destroy the enemy tanks at a range of more than 2km. A first batch of 300 Shermans was withdrawn from American tank units and sent to North Africa after Gazala. Although one of the vessels carrying them was sunk en route, by 11 September 1942 a total of 318 Shermans had been delivered.

battle. Using the capped shell, which enabled the 75mm gun to penetrate the steel-hardened armour of the German tanks, the Sherman was able to deal with them at a 2,000-metre range (the 6 pounder was mainly effective at 1,000 metres). With the Panzer definitively outgunned, not to say largely outnumbered too, the Eighth Army held the decisive advantage at Alamein.

The Tactics

Panzer Army Africa

The basic innovation in the tactics used in the Western Desert campaign was introduced by the Afrika Korps, which took best advantage of the German 'mission tactics' command system. This was based on a simple method; commanders were given orders simply stating their mission, not how to accomplish it. The high level of flexibility and manoeuvreability this system allowed was integrated by the large use of 'combat groups', formed around basic units of the divisions (like the Panzer or the infantry regiments), made up of a mixture of tanks and infantry, and integrated with anti-tank guns and artillery. Close inter-arms coordination and cooperation was also a key factor in the German Army; armour would not operate alone but in close relation with both the infantry and the artillery, in order to be able to face any possible kind of enemy unit.

These innovative tactics meant that the Germans were able to compensate for the difference between their own and the enemy tanks; a simple tactic largely used in the Western Desert saw the German tanks used as 'bait' against the British tanks. They would attack and, if outnumbered or outgunned, withdraw behind an anti-tank gun screen, which was left to deal with the enemy tanks. They would then outmanoeuvre the British tank formations, already badly mauled, attacking them in the flanks and the rear. Such tactics were quite effective not only thanks to the advantage the Germans had due to their 88mm and 76.2mm guns, but also

15. Close inspection of an abandoned German 88mm anti-aircraft and anti-tank gun, note the Thompson machine pistol carried by the soldier.

because of the ineffective British response to them. In fact, the British Army mainly relied on the 'top down' command system which, to the contrary of the German system, saw commanders issuing detailed orders to their subordinates, who had to carry them out according to plans. This greatly lessened flexibility, and a good deal of manoeuvreability, in combat, with the fatal consequence that the Germans were quicker in reacting to the British moves.

Eighth Army

The British Army greatly suffered from insufficient inter-arms cooperation; armoured formations would often attack alone without infantry (and artillery) support and, also given the fact that early British tanks only had armour piercing shells for their

16. The officer leading his men holds a Webley pistol in his hand.

main gun (practically useless against infantry and guns), they were simply unable to deal with the German anti-tank screens, which also enjoyed the protection of infantry. The opposite was true for the Eighth Army's infantry units that, all too often lacking armoured support (and adequate anti-tank guns), were easily overwhelmed by the German 'battlegroups', comprising a mixture of tanks, infantry and guns. The harsh lesson, learned during Operation Crusader, saw – in spite of the eventual victory – the loss of 40 per cent of the British armour, against the loss of 38 per cent of the enemy armour (Italians included). Such a serious shortcoming, also a consequence of faulty field communications, led to the creation of brigade groups and the use of 'Jock columns' (a rough equivalent of the German battlegroups) which, without any real change in doctrine and fighting methods, proved largely unsuccessful.

At Gazala the Eighth Army was to suffer its greatest tank defeat when the 1st Armoured Division attacked, on 12–13 June, the Afrika Korps in what has been described as a 'series of confused actions'; this led to the loss of 121 British tanks (against three German tanks), and to the eventual overrunning of the 6th New Zealand Brigade. It is hardly surprising how, following Montgomery's take over of the Eighth Army, the return to the old tactics and command methods was largely approved and appreciated. But at Alamein, Montgomery was to take full advantage of the fact that now Rommel had to fight on his terms, and was no longer able to benefit from the superior flexibility and manoeuvreability in the open that he had previously enjoyed.

Improved British tactics were a deciding factor in the Alamein battle. Montgomery's decisive influence was to avoid a battle in the open; rather, the British forces were to break through the enemy defence line and face the counterattack, this time using the anti-tank gun screen tactic against the Axis forces in order to wear them down. This was made possible thanks to the availability of better and improved tanks and anti-tank guns, but was also a decisive innovation which overturned any possible advantage Rommel may have had in the tactical field.

THE DAYS
BEFORE BATTLE

The Axis Defence Line

After the failure to break through the Eighth Army's defences at Alam Halfa, a dispirited Rommel asked permission to withdraw his army off from the Alamein positions. Depressed by having realised that his final goal of reaching Suez was now well beyond his reach, Rommel knew he was forced on the defensive and wanted to shorten his supply lines, while defending a position more suitable for the mobile warfare his army had proven to be superior in. Hitler's refusal, dictated by political reasons (abandoning ground in Egypt meant acknowledging defeat), led to the decision to defend the Alamein line. Before taking his leave of absence from Africa, Rommel left instructions as to the main feature of the Axis defences: the building of a mined main line of resistance which, in the absence of any other hindrance, was to blunt the enemy offensive. Mine laying had in fact been started already early in July, facing the first counteroffensive at El Alamein, and it was increased in September; until 20 October the German chief engineer, Colonel Hecker, estimated that a total of 445,358 mines had been laid. This figure included 249,849 anti-tank and 14,509 anti-personnel mines, plus some other 181,000-

El Alamein 1942

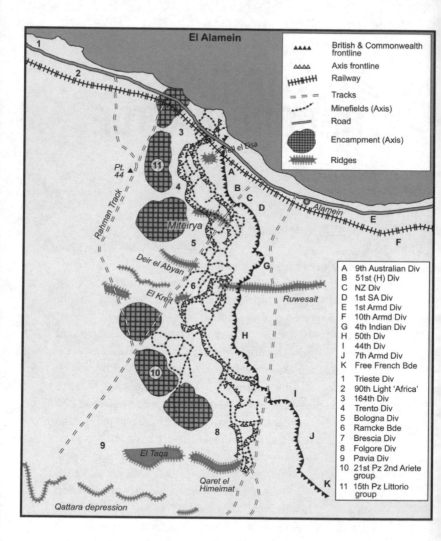

Legend:
- ▲▲▲▲ British & Commonwealth frontline
- △△△△ Axis frontline
- ╫╫╫ Railway
- — — — Tracks
- ·····— Minefields (Axis)
- —— Road
- ⬤ Encampment (Axis)
- ⚏⚏⚏ Ridges

A	9th Australian Div
B	51st (H) Div
C	NZ Div
D	1st SA Div
E	1st Armd Div
F	10th Armd Div
G	4th Indian Div
H	50th Div
I	44th Div
J	7th Armd Div
K	Free French Bde
1	Trieste Div
2	90th Light 'Africa'
3	164th Div
4	Trento Div
5	Bologna Div
6	Ramcke Bde
7	Brescia Div
8	Folgore Div
9	Pavia Div
10	21st Pz 2nd Ariete group
11	15th Pz Littorio group

Map labels: El Alamein, Tell el Eisa, Alamein, Pt. 44, Rahman Track, Miteirya, Deir el Abyan, El Kreit, Ruwesait, El Taqa, Qaret el Himeimat, Qattara depression

mine strong British minefields had been incorporated into the Axis defences following the withdrawal from Alam Halfa. These minefields had been further reinforced using some 180,000 British mines taken from captured dumps. This enabled the Panzer Army Africa to build a defence line echeloned in depth; stretching over some 37 miles (60km) from the Arab Gulf down to the Qattara Depression, the line was formed by a 500–1,000-metre deep series of outposts, followed by a 'cushion' of unmanned defences some 1–2 kilometres deep. Behind the westerly half of the minefields lay the main defence line, some 2 kilometres deep and divided in a 'chequered' series of minefields, each one identified with a letter, where the units were deployed in their dug-outs with every battalion covering an approximate 1½ kilometre wide area, up to 5 kilometres deep.

Such a defence system was designed to break the waves of the enemy attacking forces, and enable the Axis positions to support each other while the 'chequered' minefield, running east to west, prevented the enemy units from either supporting each other or even simply combining their strengths. Basically, the idea

17. *A lone Italian sentry of the Folgore Division overlooking the Qattara Depression, south of El Alamein.*

18. A German engineer laying a mine in a desert track; many of those used at Alamein came from captured British stocks.

was that the enemy forces, after they managed to break through the main line of defence, would have been counterattacked by the Axis mobile mechanised forces with the aim of blunting the offensive and restoring the defence line. This was esentially the German defence tactics, which relied on the firm protection of the main line with the aim of breaking up the attacking forces and, as soon as the 'point of main effort' of the enemy attack had been located, to counterattack it using the armoured units which, relying once more on their flexibility and manoeuvreability, would have defeated the enemy and put an end to his attack. Such a system had in fact worked already in July 1942, and the use of a heavily mined defence line could only bring further advantage to it. There were, on the other hand, other factors Rommel, and his temporary successor, had to take into account in their defence plans. The first factor was their sheer lack of manpower;

EIGHTH ARMY'S SUPPLIES

The Eighth Army required at least 10,500 tons of supplies per day of combat, including some 700 tons of rations and another 900 of water (about 5 tons of rations and 7 tons of water per division), some 900 tons of fuel for tanks and other vehicles, and 144 tons of ammunition per every single regiment of artillery.

when Operation Lightfoot started on 23 October 1942, the Axis forces had an overall strength of 152,000, 90,000 of which were Germans and 62,000 Italians (plus some other 52,000 in the rear area). These figures take into account, however, all the German and Italian personnel in the area (naval and air force included), while the actual strength of the frontline units of the army – which, in its German part, was also heavily affected by some 10,000 cases of sickness – was much lower.

Panzer Army Africa's Strength

Panzer Army Africa's actual strength was about 110,000, with 53,736 men in the German and 56,123 in the Italian units. The actual combat strength of the German units (including the four German divisions and the parachute brigade, plus corps and army troops) was 48,854, showing how these enjoyed a much more favourable 'tooth to tail' ratio. Italian combat strength was 46,174, with 15,386 men in the XXI Corps deployed to the north, 12,195 with the X Corps deployed to the south and 18,593 with the mobile XX Corps. Some other 9,949 men were deployed in the rear area, down to the Sahara, for security duties (these included the Pavia and Young Fascists divisions). Lack of infantry was one of the biggest issues, since only 13,969 German soldiers (belonging to both the 164th Division and the parachute brigade) could be deployed at the front along with the 27,581 Italians, thus giving an average strength per kilometre of about 700 men, although the actual disposition gave a much better ratio to the northern area while to the south of the Deir el Abyan, the front (occupied by the Ramcke parachute brigade and the Italian Bologna, Brescia and Folgore divisions) was only thinly held with an average strength per kilometre of about 550 men. Such a disadvantage was further aggravated by the fact that it was not possible to deploy units according to the 'corset rods' principle, which meant interposing German and Italian battalions, thereby avoiding any 'weak' (i.e. Italian-held) sections of the line, as in the northern area. There were also other serious issues: German units, regardless of their proximity to the Italian units, could not issue orders to them

19. Italian 75mm self-propelled guns in the desert; the most effective Italian armour was only available in small quantities, and was also hampered by its slow speed.

(these had to be issued by Panzer Army's command via the appropriate chain), but only at best could they submit a request. Also, the fact that most of the mines laid were anti-tank, rather than anti-personnel devices, meant that a well-organised attack could only be slowed down, but that removal of those mines was only a matter of time. Further along the line, lacking any wood or concrete, the defence positions were simple holes dug in the desert; though very hard to see from ground level (but the Royal Air Force managed to spot them thanks to air reconnaissance), they offered no protection against artillery and air attacks.

Problems also afflicted the mobile reserves; with two groups deployed in the north (15th Panzer and Littorio divisions) and in the south (21st Panzer and Ariete), it was possible to promptly face any threat from every direction although the necessary dispersion of reserves also meant that concentrating them to deliver a massive counterattack would have been a clumsy and time-consuming procedure. This was particularly true given the supply conditions of the Panzer Army; with the British naval and air interdiction of the sea lanes back into action, supplies reached Libya and Egypt only on a small scale. Fuel was the most important issue at the time; the German fuel reserves on the eve of the battle were limited to only three 'consumption units' (each estimated for a day of battle), one of which was still in Benghazi. That meant the mobile reserves could counterattack any enemy breakthrough but, once one of the two groups was moved from its positions and switched either north or south, it would have been impossible to reverse the move if necessary. This effectively meant the two groups were in fact to fight mainly as separate bodies. Tank availability was, on the other hand, another problem especially in comparison with the Allies: there was a total of 234 German tanks (plus another thirty under repair), and 289 Italian tanks and self-propelled guns (plus another ninety under repair). Quality was the main issue – thirty of the 234 German tanks were the light Panzer II type, while eighty-one were outdated short-barrelled 50mm Panzer IIIs, and eight

20. A short-barrelled 75mm Panzer IV German tank in the desert.

were short-barrelled 75mm Panzer IVs. The only modern tanks were eighty-five long-barrelled 50mm Panzer IIIs and thirty long-barrelled 75mm Panzer IVs. The 255 Italian M14/41 tanks were outdated as well (like the fourteen L6 light tanks, also available), and only the thirty-three self-propelled 75mm guns possessed a certain degree of efficiency.

This did not mean the two mobile groups were completely inefficient; the northern group included the 15th Panzer which, along with 110 operational tanks (twelve Panzer IIs, thirty-eight short-barrelled and forty-three long-barrelled Panzer IIIs, two short-barrelled and fifteen long-barrelled Panzer IVs), also had seventy 50mm anti-tank guns, eight 88mm anti-tank and anti-aircraft guns, sixteen self-propelled 76.2mm anti-tank guns, forty-one Italian guns (probably the 47/32 anti-tank), and four captured 6 pounder guns. The Littorio Division had 212 medium tanks and sixteen self-propelled guns. In the south the 21st Panzer had 124 tanks (eighteen Panzer IIs, forty-three short-barrelled and forty-two long-barrelled Panzer IIIs, six short-barrelled and fifteen long-barrelled Panzer IVs), while the Italian Ariete Division had 234 medium tanks and seventeen self-propelled guns. The large amount of anti-tank guns available partly compensated for the lack of suitable armour; the Axis forces possessed a total of 1,063 anti-tank guns which, if partly outdated and unsuitable (like the Italian 47/32 gun), also included a rather large number of German 50 and 76.2mm guns. The 164th Division had, for example, 180 of the former, while the Italian Trento Division had seventy 47/32 guns. The amount of field artillery was, on the other hand, rather poor with just 552 pieces.

German intelligence had no clear picture of the situation; according to its reports the likely areas of enemy attack were around the Deir el Munassib in the south, in the area of the Ruwesait Ridge, and to the south of the coastal road in the north. Such uncertainty certainly contributed to the splitting up of the mobile forces, although the actual disposition on the frontline suggests that a possible threat to the northern area was taken more seriously than a possible breakthrough in the south. No actual defence plan was developed; on the eve of the battle General Stumme (Rommel's replacement) had the commanders of the two Panzer divisions start a series of defence exercises based on prompt counterattacks against a breach of the defence line, but Operation Lightfoot was launched before these went beyond the planning stage.

MONTY AND ROMMEL

Although their names are often associated in the desert war, they actually faced each other on this battlefield for a relatively short period only. Montgomery took over command of the Eighth Army on 12 August 1942, one and a half years after Rommel's arrival in North Africa; Rommel left North Africa on 9 March 1943.

Eighth Army's Strength

On paper, Montgomery's Eighth Army was largely superior to the Axis forces: its total strength was more than 220,000, 195,000 of which was made up of combat units, and it had a total of 1,351 tanks (not including some other 1,000 in the workshops), 1,136 of which were with the field units. However, only 1,029 of these were serviceable with the following break down: 170 M3 Lee/Grant (fifty-nine with 10th Armoured, seventy-one with 7th Armoured and thirty-seven with 9th Armoured Brigade attached to the New Zealand Division), 252 M4 Sherman (ninety-two with 1st Armoured, 124 with 10th Armoured; thirty-six with 9th Armoured Brigade), 216 Crusader with 2 pounder gun (forty-seven with 1st Armoured, sixty-eight with 10th Armoured, forty-nine with 7th Armoured divisions, thirty-seven with 9th Armoured Brigade and fifteen with the 9th Australian Division), seventy-eight Crusader III 6 pounder guns (twenty-nine with 1st Armoured, twenty-nine with 10th Armoured and eight with 7th Armoured divisions), 119 M3 Stuart (eighty-six with 7th Armoured,

21. M3 medium Lee/Grant tanks moving in the desert; its high silhouette made it an easy target.

twenty-nine with the New Zealand and four with the Australian divisions), 194 Valentine tanks, all with the 23rd Armoured Brigade attached to the Australian, New Zealand and British 51st Infantry divisions. A total of 1,451 anti-tank guns included 554 2 pounder and 849 6 pounder guns, while 892 artillery pieces (mostly the excellent 25 pounder) outnumbered those in the Axis armoury. Air superiority, with 530 serviceable aircraft against 350 Axis aircraft (though some other 150 could be mustered from the Mediterranean bases), was attempted but not achieved.

Actual combat strength was in fact something quite different; given their unfavourable 'tooth to tail' ratio, the infantry divisions of the Eighth Army – with an overall establishment of 17,298 all ranks – were somewhat at a disadvantage since each one of their infantry brigades could only field less than 3,000 men, of which 2,358 actually were in the three infantry battalions. Since these would have been in the lead, each with four companies of 124 men, every battalion would have had an actual combat strength of about 500 men in all. Although the recent intake of some 41,000 replacements brought some units, in particular the 51st Infantry Division, to be overstrength, some others were on the other hand understrength; actual strength of the infantry battalions in the 9th Australian Division (in spite of the arrival of reinforcements on 10 October, who were not used because they could not be trained in time) ranged from 650 to 780 out of an established strength of 848, although weapons were available in large quantity. The New Zealand Division still suffered from the losses of the previous months and one of its brigades, the 4th, was being reorganised as an armoured brigade while handing over some 600 men to the two others. Given its lack of strength and replacements, the division was not deemed capable of facing sustained action, just like the 1st South African Division (itself lacking strength and due to be reorganised into the 6th Armoured Division) and the 4th Indian Division, that only had one brigade fit for offensive actions. Shifting available men was also quite impossible since, for political and organisational reasons,

22. The 2 pounder British anti-tank gun, outdated at the time of El Alamein.

men from different nationalities could only fight in their own units (thus the Greek and Free French brigades were kept as such, in spite of Montgomery's decision to concentrate only on divisions). The basic attack scheme developed by the infantry commanders also put great strain on individual companies; simplistically, the attack was to be lead by two infantry companies which, once they had seized their objective, were to shift to defence while two other fresh units were to pass through them in order to maintain momentum. Such an attack developing into four waves, while designed to bring new and fresh units forward, also meant that the first waves (those likely to face the early enemy reaction and suffer more casualties) would in fact be facing an equally strong enemy, with the unenviable perspective of being worn out during the early stages of the assault.

OPERATION BERTRAM

Led by Colonel Charles Richardson, this operation was aimed at deceiving Rommel as to the real area of the attack. Jasper Maskelyne (an officer of the engineering corps, formerly a stage magician) had tanks in the northern area masked with canvas to look like lorries, while reversing the process in the south along with creating dummy guns and dumps.

Training

Training was another major issue; British 51st (Highland) Infantry Division was sent to the Middle East in August and, having not been in combat, was allowed two months to acclimatise and train for the incoming offensive, which contributed to it becoming a very effective unit. However, this was not the norm and the other divisions, which to different degrees had been involved in the battles fought since early summer: the 9th Australian Division, which temporarily shifted its frontline positions with the units of the 51st Division to allow them to gain experience, could only take each brigade at a time out of the line for a week of intensive training. The same happened with the 1st South African Division, which only trained two of its brigades since the third was not going into action. The New Zealand Division started its own training from 18 September, when the 9th Armoured Brigade was first attached to it. At the end of the month divisional exercises were held, which were altogether successful apart from revealing problems in cooperation and coordination with the 9th Armoured Brigade which (in spite of further training and experiments) were not fully resolved, probably in part because the brigade only received its Sherman tanks on the eve of the offensive. The 1st and 10th Armoured divisions started to train in late September, facing several problems that included lack of experience with night movements, the late arrival of some of the new tanks, the need to integrate the new motor brigades into their organisation, with the latter also needing to acquire minefield clearing skills and practice. Above all, there was an almost complete lack of training in the field of tank–infantry coordination on the battlefield. On the other hand, training with mine removal practice was quite effective; since the specially converted Matilda tanks, which used a flail to detonate the mines, were neither available in large quantity nor really reliable, this was a task still to be undertaken by infantry and engineers with the old methods (though some magnetic mine detectors were available). A special training school was set up, and intensive training was undertaken for what was to be one of the main tasks on the first day of the battle.

Training, like the return to detailed planning with battles fought under a centralised command by divisional level units, was a key factor in Montgomery's view. Under Auchinleck's command the Eighth Army made an attempt to match the German's flexibility and mobility by decentralisation, mainly relying on brigade-sized units and allowing a greater degree of independence to its commanders. Following Montgomery's arrival there was a step back to the old, well-known methods. Divisional integrity was restored, like the customary 'top down' command system which, in this case, hinged around Montgomery himself who – given his lack of confidence in subordinate commanders – exercised close control over all the phases of the planning and of the combat. Well conscious of the

MINES

Different types of mines were used at Alamein: anti-tank mines were filled with three to five kilos of explosive and only detonated under the pressure of a heavy vehicle, like a tank. The anti-personnel mines were lighter and detonated either under the pressure of a single man, or if triggered by a tripwire when walking near them.

MINE CLEARING

The most effective way to remove a mine was to check the terrain using a bayonet and, when the mine was found, remove the fuse. The main problem in this task were the anti-personnel mines, like the German S-Mine which, when triggered, discharged a shrapnel-filled canister that exploded at chest height.

23. Eighth Army's 'secret weapon' in the second battle of Alamein: the American-built M4 Sherman tank.

limitations of his troops, he strongly opposed any fluid or mobile action, while emphasising accurate planning and a very simple doctrine based on close cooperation between tanks and infantry. Tanks were to be employed in large numbers with the basic aim of securing and holding the ground, provided with close support by the infantry units. A concentrated employment of armour, close infantry support and artillery firepower were, in Montgomery's view, the foundation upon which success on the battlefield was to be obtained. And this foundation was to be secured by unit reorganisation, security and intensive training, as it was written in his 30 August memorandum:

> It cannot be emphasised too strongly that successful battle operations depend on the intimate co-operation of all arms, whether in armoured or unarmoured formations. Tanks alone are never the answer; no one arm, alone and unaided can do any good in battle.

Planning for Operation Lightfoot

Actual planning for Operation Lightfoot was clearly influenced by all these factors; the first draft dated 15 September envisaged a two-pronged attack, with a main effort in the north and a minor push in the south. The strategy was based on the infantry and engineers opening passages across the enemy defences, and allowing the armour to pass through these gaps unopposed to establish a defensive perimeter 'on a ground of their own [the armour] choice' (as specified in orders for Operation Lightfoot), close to the north–south main communication tracks. Here they were to face the enemy's armoured counterattacks, thus denying Rommel any benefit from the mobile tactics he was used to, wearing down his forces in a battle of attrition, which allowed the Eighth Army an advantage because of its superiority. Lack of training, as well as the criticisms addressed to this plan by sceptical subordinate commanders concerned about its feasibility, suggested it might not have worked. This led to a revision dated 6 October which emphasised to an even greater extent the tanks– infantry cooperation; the plan, built on the basic scheme of the previous one, was based on infantry breaking into the enemy

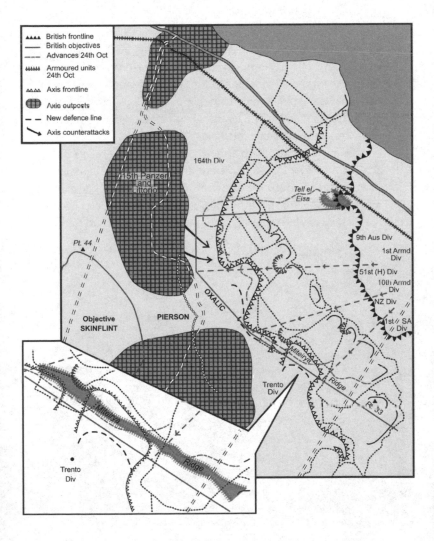

defences (this time with the main effort in the north, the southern prong being mainly reduced to a feint) and the armoured formations passing through them to form a screen to face the enemy armour. This would separate the enemy armour from the enemy infantry which, in the meantime, could be destroyed by Eighth Army's infantry formations and the breach on their northern and southern shoulders widened further. Deprived of a defensive line, what was left of Rommel's mobile reserves – already depleted by having counterattacked Eighth Army's armoured units – could then be easily destroyed in the field.

In its actual layout, the plan envisaged a 10-mile (16km) wide attack by the four infantry divisions under XXX Corps' command (from north to south: 9th Australian, 51st, New Zealand and 1st South African), each moving into a 3.5km wide corridor that was to be cleared from mines in order to create two further

24. A column of Valentine tanks crossing a mine-cleared lane at Alamein; congestion was one of the main problems Eighth Army's units faced in the early stages of Operation Lightfoot.

corridors (each one about 1.5km wide) to the north and to the south through which the 1st and 10th Armoured divisions were to pass. Infantry units were to reach the 'Oxalic Line' (running approximately from the Kidney Ridge to the Miteirya Ridge), penetrate some 2.5–5km deep into the enemy defence line, and establish themselves there. The armour were to reach the 'Pierson Line', which was just some 1.5–3km beyond the Oxalic Line. Once both lines had been reached and secured, by dawn on 24 October, a 'dog fight' was to ensue (and last for about a week) during which the enemy infantry would have been dislodged from its positions and destroyed, while the bulk of the enemy armoured and mobile forces' counterattacks would have been defeated by Eighth Army's armour and anti-tank weapons. The subsequent breakout and advance to the objective 'Skinflint', right across the Rahman track running north–south around Point 44 (Tell el Aqqaqir), would have ensured the definitive destruction of what was left of the enemy forces.

On the eve of the battle, Montgomery issued an order of the day that clearly stated the aim to 'destroy Rommel and his Army':

> The battle which is now about to begin will be one of the decisive battles of history. It will be the turning point of the war. The eyes of the whole world will be on us, watching anxiously which way the battle will swing.

SPECIAL MATILDA TANKS

Called the 'Scorpion', the Matilda flail tank was equipped with protruding arms in front of the hull where a series of chains, tied to a cylinder, were rotated by an engine (prone to breakdowns) to detonate mines. Matilda CDL (canal defence light), a battalion of which was intended to take part in Alamein, was equipped with a searchlight.

THE BATTLEFIELD:
WHAT ACTUALLY HAPPENED?

The Break-in

Operation Lightfoot commences, Axis
defences are attacked in the north and the south.

23 October	**9.40pm**	XXX Corps' artillery opens fire on Axis artillery positions
	9.55pm	Infantry of XXX Corps' units reaches the start line
	10pm	XXX Corps' artillery starts its barrage on the Axis frontline; XIII Corps attacks in the south
	10.07pm	XXX Corps' infantry starts to advance
	11pm	Axis units are alarmed

Right before dusk the British and Commonwealth units of XXX Corps, like those of X Corps behind them and the XIII Corps in the south, started to move to their forward positions each following a familiar pattern; every battalion formed for the night movement and the assault with the two leading companies followed by battalion HQ and the two follow-up companies. Since every unit was expected to be able to fight for at least 24 hours without any hope of resupply, infantry soldiers were well laden; each one carried, apart from the usual small pack with a white St Andrews cross on it to aid recognition in the darkness, an extra weight including 50 rounds of ammunition, two hand grenades, Hawkins mines and four sandbags. While the men lay down in wait and the tank crews started the engines of their vehicles, at 9:40pm on 23 October the 457 artillery pieces of XXX Corps started the first part of their heavy bombardment that was to last for about 5½ hours. The first target, the enemy artillery and gun positions, was hit for 15 minutes with incredible precision and accurate timing. Such a concentration of fire had partly been made possible by a simple trick used to synchronise fire from all the artillery batteries: using the BBC radio signal to check their watches. Meanwhile, RAF bombers dropped about 125 tons of bombs on their targets. At 9.55pm the firing stopped and, while the soldiers moved to the start lines and prepared to jump forward at zero hour, at 10pm the artillery started to fire again, this time delivering a precise barrage on the enemy positions ahead of the Eighth Army's units. After 7 minutes of fire, the barrage started to lift forward, following different patterns for each one of the divisional advance lanes.

When the sound of exploding shells began to move away, the spearheading units of the four infantry divisions started to advance: the battle had begun. Every division attacked in line, on a two-brigade front with the third brigade following up, along with the armoured support provided by the battalions of the 23rd Brigade

ARTILLERY AT EL ALAMEIN, PART ONE

Eighth Army's artillery enjoyed superiority not only in guns, but also in ammunition. During the battle the field guns fired an average of 102 rounds per day, for a total of 1,008,500 rounds, while medium guns fired an average of 140 per day, for a total of some 83,500.

25. A Valentine tank carried by a Scammell tractor.

equipped with their Valentine tanks (each one with the 9th
Australian, 51st and 1st South African divisions), while the entire
9th Armoured Brigade supported the 2nd New Zealand Division.
As the soldiers moved forward, checking the enemy and the mines,
it became clear that the men of the Panzer Army Africa had been
taken completely by surprise. There were no great difficulties
in overcoming the German and Italian outposts and soon the
spearheading units reached the main line of resistance. As recalled
by Captain Grant Murray, 5th Seaforth Highlanders (152nd Brigade,
51st Infantry Division):

> To our front all was quiet apart from a Verey light or two and
> some machine-gun fire. As zero drew near I twisted round and
> looked back towards our lines. Suddenly the whole horizon
> went pink and for a second or two there was still perfect
> silence, and then the noise of 8th Army's guns hit us in a solid
> wall of sound, that made the whole earth shake. Through the
> din we made out other sounds – the whine of shells overhead,
> the clatter of the machine guns… and eventually the pipes.
> Then we saw a sight that will live for ever in our memories – line

upon line of steel-helmeted figures with rifles at the high port, bayonets catching in the moonlight, and over all the wailing of the pipes… As they passed they gave us the thumb-up sign, and we watched them plod on towards the enemy lines, which by this time were shrouded in smoke. Our final sight of them was just as they entered the smoke, with the enemy's defensive fire falling among them.

From Carver, *El Alamein*, p.99

In the sector of the 9th Australian Division, stretching south of the Tell el Eisa station, things went rather smoothly; while on the right wing of the division a composite force advanced to protect the northern flank, the division advanced with the 26th Brigade on the right and the 20th on the left. Ten minutes after midnight their leading battalions had reached the first objectives, with just 15 minutes delay, and at 12.55 on 24 October the follow-up units took over the lead. In the 26th Brigade area some enemy resistance was encountered, along with some problems due to anti-personnel mines; however, some 15 minutes before 4am the spearheading companies reached the positions on the Oxalic Line and started to dig in. Things did not go so smoothly in the 20th Brigade sector; leading companies ran into strong German-held positions and, while still trying to clear the deep minefields, a fierce struggle started. With the leading companies pinned down in front of the German positions, the order to withdraw and reorganise was eventually given and at dawn the brigade's leading battalion was still about 1km short of the Oxalic Line.

The 51st (Highland) Division in the midst of its baptism of fire, was also advancing on the wider lane stretching for about 2.5km; on the right flank the 153rd Brigade (with the 5th Black Watch leading), moving forward at the sound of the bagpipes, immediately ran into heavy enemy resistance from a battalion of the German 164th Division. The same fate occurred to the leading battalions of the 154th Brigade, with the consequence that heavy casualties were suffered, and some of the leading companies were

26. Clearing lanes across the Axis minefields at El Alamein was a time-consuming and complicated procedure, even after the battle was over.

down to a strength of some sixty men. At dawn the two brigades were still short of their final objectives on the Oxalic Line, with the 154th closer to them on the left wing, but with the 153rd Brigade held far behind. Although the division overall performed well, the troubles with 153rd Brigade were to cause a considerable delay in opening the corridor through which the 1st Armoured Division was supposed to move, right across the southern and northern shoulders of the 9th Australian and 51st divisions. The 2nd New Zealand and the 1st South African divisions shared a common objective, the Miteirya Ridge which formed the southern shoulder of the whole front; the New Zealanders' advance was carried out by the 5th Brigade on the right and the 6th on the left; here too leading battalions ran into difficulties, namely enemy resistance and minefields, but at dawn both brigades had managed to secure positions behind the ridge close to the Oxalic Line, with the exception of the 6th Brigade's 28th (Maori) Battalion that ran into heavier enemy resistance and was held up before the ridge. 1st South African Division, allotted a smaller section of the front and mainly tasked with securing the left wing of the offensive, was not as successful; resistance from an Italian battalion and minefields delayed the advance of the 2nd Brigade on the right wing, which reached the Miteirya Ridge but fell short of the Oxalic Line objectives while, on the left, the 3rd Brigade (facing no enemy positions) eventually reached the line a few minutes past 5am.

While infantry advanced through the minefields and the enemy positions, at 2am on 24 October the two armoured divisions of the X Corps started to move from their assembly areas; in order to reach their objectives on the Pierson Line by dawn, there was a problem to face: clearing adequately large gaps through the minefields and, in some points, even further than the infantry had actually advanced. Mine clearing was a key factor in the advance since only a few Scorpion flail tanks were available, and most of those used quickly broke down, thus ensuring that the ordinary soldier had to take responsibility for checking for mines in the ground using a bayonet. In the majority of cases the advancing infantry had been able to clear gaps through the minefields, but this took more time than expected and in some cases the task was not complete, like at Miteirya where no breach was made on and beyond the ridge. Out of the six lanes each armoured division was intended to make only one in the northern corridor, the 1st Armoured Division actually reached the infantry's advanced positions by dawn on 24 October. Other lanes for the division had only been half cleared, while only those of the 10th Armoured Division stretched up to the Miteirya Ridge. 1st Armoured Division moved on with the 2nd Armoured Brigade in the lead followed by the 7th Motor Brigade, which was to deploy on the right wing, while the 10th Armoured Division advanced with the 9th Armoured Brigade on the right and the 8th on the left. Yet, in spite of the plan that envisaged a breakthrough to the Pierson Line before dawn, at first light on 24 October the 2nd Armoured Brigade was still some 3 miles (5km) short of it, while 8th Armoured Brigade's attempt to move beyond Miteirya Ridge was met by anti-tank fire and the still uncleared minefields, with the consequence that the brigade shifted to defence positions behind the ridge. All other brigades reached at dawn, more or less, the same positions they were intended to reach during the night.

ARTILLERY AT EL ALAMEIN, PART TWO

Compared to other battles, Eighth Army's artillery concentration at Alamein of thirty-one guns per km was rather poor; at Cassino this was 127 guns per km, and in Normandy (Operation Goodwood) 259. In the First World War there were 92 guns per km on the Somme, 125 at Cambrai and 160 during the final assault in 1918.

The Axis Reaction

Eighth Army's infantry reaches the Oxalic Line, but armoured thrusts are halted on open ground. The attack is called off in the south.

24 October	00.10am	XXX Corps' leading units reach their objectives
	1am	The second wave of XXX Corps' infantry takes the lead
	2am	X Corps' two armoured divisions start to move from assembly areas
	2.30am	In the south, 7th Armoured Division clears gaps in the enemy minefields
	3.45am	The first leading infantry companies reach their objectives on the Oxalic Line
	4am	In the south a bridgehead is established by 7th Armoured Division on the Axis minefields
	5am	The last advancing units halt at the positions just before the Oxalic Line
	6.30am	The commander of German 15th Panzer Division orders to counterattack
	9am	The Germans restore the frontline
	9.45am	General Montgomery orders XXX Corps to clear the corridor for the advancing armour of X Corps
	3.25pm	A tank squadron of 1st Armoured Division moves into open ground past the infantry, quickly halted by German anti-tank gun fire
	10pm	German air raid hits 8th Brigade's assembly area, causing loss of vehicles and attracting more German fire on other assembly areas
	10.30pm	New attempt by 7th Armoured Division to break through the enemy lines in the south

No sign of the imminent attack was detected by Panzer Army Africa, and the artillery bombardment – and the following start of the offensive – came as a great surprise; at 11pm Axis units were alarmed but soon, because of the heavy shelling, communications broke down. Only at midnight did it become apparent that this was the long-awaited offensive. The experience on the other side is described by Captain Ralf Klinger, an infantry company commander with the 21st Panzer Division:

> The 'Inferno' came with a bang – with an inhuman relentless series of explosions. The whole desert horizon seemed to burn and to shudder. As I surfaced from a deep sleep, the shock raced through my limbs – the bang was like a battering ram, no, it was the Moloch, the superhuman enemy. It drummed, the explosions were so frequent that one couldn't distinguish them singly. The shells howled overhead and exploded, the ground rocked and the detonations shook me into confusion. I felt a shiver going up my spine… No one knew what was up. We could only hope and wait in our miserable foxholes, out of contact with our battalions headquarters.
>
> from Forty, *Afrika Korps at War: The Long Road Back*, p.73

Not even by dawn had a clear picture of the situation been obtained and Rommel's temporary replacement, General Stumme, decided to reach the frontline along with the army communication staff officer but, during the journey, the car was shot at; Stumme died of a heart attack and fell from the vehicle, while the staff officer was mortally wounded. Since Stumme's body was not recovered until the following day, the uncertainty was further aggravated and the Afrika Korps' commander, General Wilhelm von Thoma, took over temporary command. Meanwhile, the situation became clearer; in the northern area (in the Australian sector and the northern shoulder of the 51st Division's area) two Italian battalions of the Trento Division, along with a German battalion of the 164th, had been overrun, while to the south, along the Miteirya Ridge where another Italian battalion had been overtaken, positions were still being held to the south of the ridge. Already at a quarter past midnight the Panzer Army Africa ordered to prepare to

27. A German command unit with motorcycles and a command Panzer III tank; note the captured British vehicle in the background.

counterattack the enemy, but it was only at 6.30am that General Gustav von Vaerst, the commander of 15th Panzer Division, ordered his division to start the counterattack to prevent an enemy breakthrough and to try and restore the situation. Immediately, elements from one combat group moved towards the more threatened areas in the Australian and 51st Division sectors with a mixture of infantry and tanks units and, by 9am, the frontline had been restored; the same happened on the northern end of the Miteirya Ridge where a 3.7-mile (6km) gap had been torn by the New Zealanders, followed by the tanks of 8th Armoured Brigade. The first clashes between the German and British armour soon revealed new problems; until then the Germans were used to firing at long range, about 2km, against the British armour, whose replies were ineffective. On 24 October, during the first clash with the Sherman tanks, the Germans were greatly surprised to be fired upon at long range, this time with great effectiveness.

At 9.45am on 24 October General Montgomery ordered XXX Corps to clear the corridor and, specifically, the New Zealand Division to exploit southwards from Miteirya Ridge supported by the 10th Armoured Division, which was to break through to the Pierson Line along with 1st Armoured. Meanwhile the 9th Australian Division was to plan a 'crumbling operation' (a shock tactic using fire and infantry to weaken enemy defensive positions one by one, thus 'crumbling' the line) for the following night. On the ground, it was quite clear why the first stage of Operation Lightfoot had not really gone according to plan: the infantry was reluctant to attack in broad daylight, while the confusion created by having deployed so many units in such a narrow, crammed space further aggravated the already chaotic situation created by the clearing of the minefields and the problems commanders faced in determining exactly where their units were (quite a hard task in a featureless terrain like the desert). In the afternoon of 24 October, at 3.25pm, a squadron of the 9th Lancers (part of 1st Armoured Division, 2nd Brigade) moved forward into open ground, soon met by the anti-tank fire of the German guns and that of the tanks of 15th Panzer Division's second battalion of the 8th Panzer Regiment; they claimed the destruction of twelve enemy tanks at the cost of four of their Shermans, but advanced no further. 10th Hussars, part of the same unit, took the best out of its Sherman tanks by using indirect fire against German tanks:

> The tank com[man]d[er] had his tank some way back from a low ridge and he himself stood on the top of the tank from which he could see the target. He then engaged the enemy target giving fire orders in the same way as for H.[igh] E.[xplosive] shooting. The result of this was that he knocked out and burnt five German tanks in the course of one afternoon and for an average of about six rounds per tank.
>
> from Barr, *Pendulum of War*, p.339

For its part the 15th Panzer Division claimed some twenty-eight enemy tanks destroyed during the day, but with the loss (either destroyed or damaged) of twenty of its own. It was quite clear that this was to be a battle of attrition.

The 'Dog Fight'

The 'dog fight' ensues, 9th Australian Division swings north.

25 October		
	3.30am	General Gatehouse asks Montgomery to halt the attack; a conference is held and Montgomery decides to pursue the attack
	3.50am	At about this time XXX and X Corps' units start to advance west
	7am	Advancing British brigades withdraw behind Miteirya Ridge
	Afternoon	Rommel, shortly arrived in Africa, analyses the situation and at 9pm the next day orders 21st Panzer Division to move north
	Night	The Eighth Army starts to regroup for the new offensive
	Midnight	9th Australian Division switches north and attacks Point 29

XXX and X corps' divisions resumed their advances at night, with mixed results; 51st Division's brigades pushed forward with a series of small-scale attacks, under constant fire from the enemy positions. Already proved by their earlier advance, the battalions made slow progress and it was not until the night of 26 October that the Oxalic Line was reached along the entire divisional front. Just to the north the 20th Australian Brigade jumped forward trying to reach the Oxalic Line, an objective which eventually they claimed before dawn but not without incident; armour from the 40th Royal Tank Regiment mistook the 'Aussies' for Germans and opened fire on them – just one of the many hiccups created by the difficulties of determining the actual position of the units.

A more serious accident was to occur with both the 1st and 10th Armoured divisions; thanks to the clearing of lanes through the minefields, 1st Armoured Division's 7th Motor Rifle Brigade was able to move to the frontline only to be unable to disperse its vehicles and men. As a result these targets soon drew fire from

EL ALAMEIN VICTORIA CROSSES

First to be awarded the Victoria Cross, Britain's highest
bravery medal, was Percival Eric (Percy) Gratwick, born 1902
in Katanning, Western Australia. A private in 2/48th Battalion,
26th Brigade, on the night of 25–26 October, he was to charge
alone a German machine gun pit on Miteirya Ridge, being
eventually killed by a second machine gun.

the enemy, with costly consequences. Worse fate was met by the
10th Armoured Division which, during the night, reorganised along
with the 9th Armoured Brigade to attack beyond the Miteirya
Ridge (9th Brigade was left with only two battalions, since the 9th
Royal Wiltshire Yeomanry handed over its seven remaining tanks to
the other two); mine clearing was, once more, a long and difficult
task and it slowed down any possible movement. Also, at 10pm
on 24 October, a German air raid hit the assembly area of the 8th
Armoured Brigade with lethal consequences: vehicles started to
burn, and the light attracted even more German bombers and
artillery fire, which also hit the assembly areas of the 9th and
24th brigades. The necessary, hurried dispersion of the tanks
and the vehicles generated much confusion and further slowed
down the movement. Eventually, General Alexander Gatehouse,
the divisional commander, acting on advice from his brigade
commander, decided to halt the advance beyond the ridge since
the division was no longer able to keep up with the artillery fire,
and there was a danger that it may have been vulnerable to enemy
reaction in broad daylight, with all its units largely disorganised and
fully exposed on the southern slope of the ridge.

Gatehouse's request to halt the attack reached Montgomery's
HQ and, at 3.30am on 25 October, a conference was held to
analyse the situation; having heard both XXX and X corps'
commanders, Montgomery decided there were chances for
the attack, a decision also motivated by a series of inaccurate

information. In fact, it had been (incorrectly) reported to Montgomery that 9th Armoured Brigade was already through the minefields' gaps, moving south-west, while 24th Brigade was already clearing the gaps and would have been through by daylight, soon followed by the 8th Brigade, although this was 'somewhat disorganised'. In a heated conversation on the field telephone between Montgomery and Gatehouse, usually reported in accounts with at least two different versions, the former gave the final order to continue with the attack, but some confusion clearly arose and still at 3.50am no obvious order had been given to the units on the field. Roughly at the same time, 24th Brigade had started to pass through the gaps and to advance west, eventually to report at dawn that it had reached the Pierson Line – which, in fact, it had not, being still about 1km short of it. 8th Armoured Brigade followed up, following the tanks of 24th Brigade less than a kilometre away, while 9th Brigade was by then halfway to its objective and, to the rear, the 133rd Lorried Infantry Brigade was pushing forward to the Miteirya Ridge, even though this added further congestion and confusion to an already overcrowded area. At dawn the tanks of 8th Armoured Brigade came under intense anti-tank fire from the battlegroup of the German 15th Panzer Division, well hidden in their pits. The British tanks were hit on their turrets, where most of

EL ALAMEIN VICTORIA CROSSES, PART TWO

Second to be awarded the VC at El Alamein was British Lieutenant Colonel Victor Buller Turner, born in Reading (Berkshire) in 1942 he commanded the 2nd Battalion, The Rifle Brigade, of 7th Motor Brigade. On 27 October, attacking 'Woodcock', he faced German armoured counterattacks and destroyed five tanks manning a 6 pounder gun.

28. A line up of M4 Sherman tanks ready to get into action.

the ammunitions were stowed, the Shermans started to explode and burst into flames, an 'unforgettable nightmare' for the men involved in this clash. At about 7am the brigade withdrew behind the ridge, and 9th Armoured Brigade (lacking fuel) would have followed if only it had not been ordered to maintain its positions. Left alone in the open, the 24th Armoured Brigade soon attracted enemy anti-tank fire, and even though the Sherman fired back it quickly became clear that, with no chances of either finding cover or resupplying in the open, there was no real opportunity to advance any further. Eventually, at dusk both the 24th and the 9th brigades withdrew behind the Miteirya Ridge.

Already before 7am on 25 October, the HQ of 15th Panzer Division had been able to correctly identify the attacks of both the 1st and 10th Armoured divisions, and – possessing full knowledge (thanks to captured documents) of Eighth Army's objectives, as given by the Oxalic Line and 'Skinflint' – ordered to stand fast and moved forward its anti-tank units, followed by its own Panzers. News of another Italian battalion overrun on the Miteirya Ridge was soon followed by a report concerning a German battalion, that had collapsed under pressure from both the 51st Infantry and 1st Armoured divisions. Since the minefields no longer offered any protection, the last available reserves were thrown into the battle to contain the advance of both 1st and 10th Armoured divisions and armoured counterattacks were launched. The 1st Armoured Division's experience was less traumatic, even if not more successful, than that of the 10th Armoured Division; 2nd Armoured Brigade started to advance west at dawn on 25 October, but it was soon under heavy fire from the German anti-tank guns which quickly destroyed six Shermans of the Queen's Bays, although losses were somewhat counterbalanced by the excellent shot fired from a Sherman of the 9th Lancers that managed to hit and destroy a single Panzer IV at a range of about 2.4 miles (4km). Still some 1km short of the Pierson Line, which the brigade thought they had already reached instead, 2nd Armoured Brigade was joined by the 7th Motor Rifle Brigade later in the morning but, during the early afternoon, both came under attack by the 15th Panzer Division's battlegroup, supported by the tanks of the Italian Littorio Division. British infantry dug in and, thanks to the skilled use of the 6 pounder anti-tank guns, were able to halt this counterattack. It was soon followed a few hours later by another one hitting both brigades; eventually, when it was called off the 7th Motor Rifle Brigade claimed the destruction of at least fourteen enemy tanks, while the 2nd Armoured Brigade claimed some thirty-nine to the loss of twenty-four of its own.

The 'fog of war', uncertainty about actual events on the battlefield, was not only due to chaos, confusion and the long range over which the tank and gun duels were fought, but also to the thick clouds of smoke, dust and sand:

> Even before reaching the enemy minefields, the dust begins to make itself felt. Gradually at first, then with increasing intensity, a heavy choking fog builds up as the tracks churns the desert into powder. When all the tanks are on the move this fog is blinding as well as physically unpleasant. Visibility is only a few yards and it is all the drivers can do to keep in touch with the tank ahead of them.
>
> from Barr, *Pendulum of War*, p.322

29. *The new 6 pounder anti-tank gun, a very effective and decisive weapon at El Alamein (to the right the charred remains of a German Panzer IV tank).*

Unsurprisingly, German 15th Panzer Division's claims suggested quite a different picture; against a loss of about twenty-five of its own tanks (which, including the Italian tanks, makes British claims quite accurate), the division claimed the destruction of no less than 119 enemy tanks, both from the 1st and the 10th Armoured divisions. The bright point was that, facing a situation not much different from that of the 10th Division, the units of the 1st Armoured Division did not withdraw but maintained their positions.

In spite of this, the situation on 25 October was not very satisfactory from Montgomery's point of view; although infantry had managed to reach the Oxalic Line all along the positions, neither armoured divisions had been able to break through the enemy defence to reach the Pierson Line and even his short-term plans were compelled to face the reality of the situation on the ground. The 2nd New Zealand Division's commander, General Bernard Freyberg, who was expected to start a 'crumbling operation' beyond Miteirya Ridge, painted a clear picture of the situation: crammed in a small space and still somehow disorganised after the attack, its units faced difficulties to reorganise, and in particular the 5th New Zealand Brigade could not be easily replaced in its positions by the 133rd Lorried Brigade. Furthermore, given the failure of both armoured divisions to break through the enemy lines and reach the Pierson Line by dawn on 24 October, which would have ensured that the Germans could not put on any anti-tank gun screens, it was clear that any further advance (now, with the enemy already on the alert and with its reserves committed) would simply mean the possible repetition of British tank crews' worst nightmare: an attack against enemy guns which had been fateful in the past (and which, in this occasion, might have cost some 500 tanks each division, according to estimates). Shortly after noon, 25 October, Montgomery had a change of heart and revised his plans: the New Zealand attack, clearly too costly against every possible advantage it might bring,

30. *A column of Italian light tanks in the desert; note the use of sandbags in the attempt to increase armour protection.*

GENERAL FREYBERG

Lieutenant General Bernard Cyril Freyberg was born in Richmond, Surrey, 1889, and raised in New Zealand. During the First World War, an officer in the British Army, he took part in the Gallipoli campaign and was awarded the Victoria Cross on the Western Front. Given command of the New Zealand Division in 1939, he kept it until 1945.

was cancelled and the whole weight of the offensive was to switch north; the two armoured divisions of X Corps were to press on to the west and the north-west of the bridgehead formed by the infantry divisions, still pushing toward the Pierson Line. Meanwhile, the 9th Australian Division was to widen its own 'crumbling operation' by swinging north, striking toward the coast in order to distract the enemy. However, unknown to 'Monty', that same afternoon Field Marshal Rommel, who had been ordered by Hitler to get back to Africa and take over command, had arrived to take the lead of his Panzer Army once more.

The 'Dog Fight' Continues: Action at 'Snipe' and 'Woodcock'

German counterattacks against the Australians; British attacks against 'Woodcock' and 'Snipe' objectives.

26 October		
	2.30pm	Rommel commits the 90th Light 'Africa' Division against the 9th Australian Division in the north
	11pm	British attacks against positions Woodcock and Snipe start

In the southern sector, the role of British XIII Corps in the early stage of Lightfoot was to launch a diversionary attack against the positions held by the Italian Folgore Division. This was mainly meant to distract enemy attention from the main front and prevent

The Battlefield: What Actually Happened?

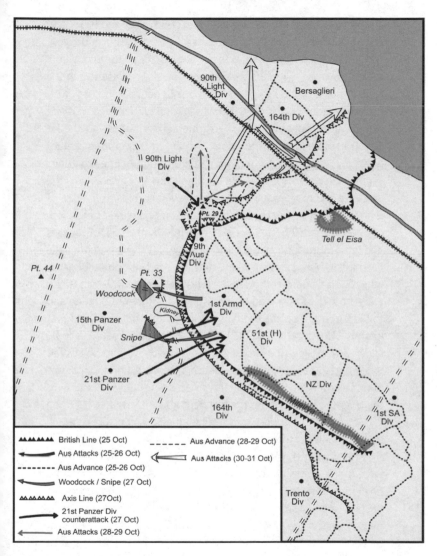

any redeployment of both the German 21st Panzer and the Italian Ariete divisions. It was made clear that the leading British division, 7th 'Desert Rats' Armoured, was not to be exposed to serious tank losses. However, given the weakness of the enemy defences in the area, it was reckoned that this attack might actually succeed, with the 7th Armoured Division eventually advancing to the Jebel Kalakh plateau just in front of the two Axis armoured divisions. Also, the 1st Free French Brigade was to attack and seize the important height of Naqb Rala, on the southernmost tip of the El Alamein defence line. Lacking both the strength and the resources available to the XXX and X corps, the XIII Corps faced several problems in spite of the thinner, and scarcely defended, enemy line lying ahead; lack of adequate artillery support was matched by the lack of sappers and infantry, making an assault like that of XXX Corps impossible. The plan was thus limited to an attack by 22nd Armoured Brigade, which was to breach the enemy lines on a some 3.7-mile (6km) wide area, to be followed by the 4th Light Armoured Brigade and to be supported on the left flank by 44th Infantry Division's 131st Infantry Brigade, while on the right flank a smokescreen was to be laid by the artillery. Paths across the minefields were to be cleared by a specially organised force and by the 44th Reconnaissance (Recce) Regiment, equipped with six Scorpion tanks. Along with the offensive in the north, the southern attack started at 10pm on 23 October and soon ran into trouble: the Scorpions broke down one after another after about one hour, and the mine-clearing task was taken over by infantry. By 2.30am on 25 October two gaps were made across the minefields, and by 4am a bridgehead had been formed by units of 44th Recce Regiment and 22nd Armoured Brigade. The attack ran head-on into the outposts held by a battlegroup of the Folgore Division, which reacted using familiar tactics: enemy forces were left to advance beyond the defence posts, only to be attacked from the rear.

With the arrival of daylight, attempts by mine-clearing teams to create a gap in the second line of minefields to the west of the outposts also ran into Italian opposition, and they were eventually forced to give up. 22nd Armoured and 131st Infantry brigades were thus holding a bridgehead leading to nowhere, which had already cost some 380 casualties. Colonel Hugh Brassey, squadron commander in the 4th Light Armoured Brigade, recalled the situation:

> After a bit our column was halted and shells started to drop around us... I was told that Nos 1 and 2 gap were going very slowly, and Nos 3 and 4 gap were blocked... At last, when I was almost in despair, we moved forward about 300 yards and I could see the entrances of 3 and 4 gaps... an 11th Hussars subaltern, acting as Traffic Controller, strolled up through a couple of shell bursts and informed me No. 3 gap was blocked by a blown-up Honey [tank] and a Carrier. So we had to halt there for about 20 minutes until it was cleared. In No. 3 gap, a squadron of 40 Carriers went in, and four got to the other side [of the minefield]: there is no doubt that the Folgore fought very well indeed that night and the 44th Recce had a very bad time.
>
> From Forty, *Desert Rats at War. North Africa* (1975), p.161

The situation worsened during the day when, in spite of the smokescreen laid to hide the movement of the 1st Free French Brigade, its advance to the Naqb Rala was spotted and the Italians welcomed them with a hail of fire; the advance of the French force was checked at first and, with daylight, it fell under heavy fire and was eventually also counterattacked by an armoured cars platoon of the 21st Panzer Division until the order to withdraw was given. A new attempt to break through the second line of minefields was made at 10.30pm on 24 October, with 131st Brigade advancing under the protection of a heavy artillery barrage; the enemy reaction, and the lack of manpower, only led to a small bridgehead through which the leading armour of 22nd Armoured Brigade tried to pass and exploit. Stubborn Italian opposition, in spite of the unsuitability of the available anti-tank guns, the intervention of elements of the 21st Panzer Division and the narrowness of

31. A light M3 Stuart (or 'Honey') tank moving past a destroyed German Panzer III medium tank.

the gaps cleared across the minefield brought a quick decision to postpone any further attempt to break through, even if with daylight on 25 October it became clear that the enemy fire could be easily subdued, and the whole attack had to be called off. This was a decision Montgomery did not approve, instead he ordered 7th Armoured Division to remain in the southern flank; thus the units of 22nd Armoured and 131st Infantry brigades held the bridgehead between the two minefields during the entire day, fully exposed to enemy fire, and not before the following night did they withdraw leaving behind small groups that were captured in the morning of 27 October. That put an end to any attempt to break through the enemy defence line by XIII Corps, even though small and large-scale raids were made to keep the enemy on the alert.

The 21st Panzer Division, forming along with the Italian Ariete, the southern mobile defence force, promptly reacted to the attacks in the area; apart from sending an armoured car unit against the Free French forces, a small group made of a company of engineers, one anti-tank and one artillery battery, along with two Italian infantry companies, reinforced the Folgore Division against the attacks of the 7th Armoured and 44th Infantry divisions. Two infantry battalions were also deployed on the line, for safety. Shortly after his arrival in Egypt in the afternoon of 25 October, Rommel evaluated the situation and identified the key factor: the lack of supplies, in particular fuel, that prevented his forces from conducting any large-scale movement or operation. After a day, he was to make a crucial decision: at 9pm on 26 October he ordered the bulk of 21st Panzer Division (leaving behind a small 'security group') to move north, to reinforce the 15th Panzer and the Littorio divisions. The Italian Ariete was to remain in the south to cover the area and provide further reinforcements, if needed. Given the lack of fuel, this order could not be reversed. The division moved at once, and about 7am on the 27th it started to deploy to face the XXX and X corps in the north.

In the northern area, the situation was still somewhat confused; while the 9th Australian Division reorganised to switch to the north, the 51st Infantry Division pushed forward with a series of small-scale attacks. During the night of 25 October the 5th Black Watch attacked the position codenamed 'Stirling' after a large-scale artillery barrage that lasted for three hours; eventually, the only fire they had to face was from their own artillery, the position being seized by dawn on the 26th without problems since it was only occupied by dead or dying Germans. The Black Watch dug in, along with anti-tank guns and a squadron from 50th Royal Tank Regiment, but during the following day they had to face intense mortar fire and sniping from the Germans. 7th Argyll and Sutherland Highlanders also attacked the position 'Nairn', this time facing heavy machine gun fire from the Germans that caused numerous casualties, so heavy in fact that two companies had to be merged together into a single one. Although these attacks enabled the 51st Division to reach its ultimate objective, they revealed the crisis that the Eighth Army was currently facing: pushing forward was actually possible, but only at the price of heavy casualties that reduced the actual combat strength of the divisions. The battle of attrition was now being fought, but it was not clear how it might turn into an advantage for the British and Commonwealth forces. On 26 October Montgomery was to face some revealing facts: so far the haul of prisoners had been relatively light, with only 628 Germans and 1,534 Italians, for a total estimate of about 1,700 German and 1,955 Italian soldiers killed, wounded and missing. Compared to Eighth Army's losses these were somewhat depressing: since 23 October the estimates gave a total of 6,140 killed, wounded or missing mainly from XXX Corps' units (4,640 in total), and only partly from either the XIII (1,040) and the X Corps (460). Losses were particularly heavy amongst infantry units, and most notably amongst their infantry brigades and battalions: 9th Australian Division had lost some 1,000 men, as had the 2nd New Zealand, while 51st Division lost some 2,000 and the 1st South African around 600. Also, approximately 300 British tanks had been put out of action even though most of them could be recovered and repaired, to be brought sooner or later back into service (X Corps had ninety-three of them under repair at the time). Axis tank losses were about 127, with the main defending force – the German 15th Panzer Division –

32. The early version of the long-barrelled 75mm Panzer IV German tank; very effective but also scarcely available at El Alamein.

33. Two German Panzer IV tanks with the short-barrelled 75mm gun, it was outdated at the time of El Alamein.

being down to a mere forty-seven tanks (including eight light Panzer IIs, but also with sixteen long-barrelled Panzer IIIs and six long-barrelled Panzer IVs), hardly a match for the some 500 operational tanks that X Corps could throw into the battle.

The real problem was a lack of replacements and reserves, and this greatly reduced Montgomery's capability to handle his divisions and adequately operate against Rommel's, in a manner to defeat them once and for all. The 2nd New Zealand Division, already understrength and lacking replacements, could only be used in one major assault again, likewise the 2nd South Africans, who were even more understrength, leaving few options. Montgomery had to rely on the 51st Infantry Division, which was already depleted and facing the hard task of widening the breach in front of the Oxalic Line, and on the men of 9th Australian Division, who in theory possessed more experience, but who were less proven. There was no margin for error – a simple mistake could result in fatal losses that might definitively break down the combat units still available and prevent any possible attempt to break out. At this point, the future Supercharge operation started to take form: Montgomery pulled the 10th Armoured Division

'CORPS DE CHASSE'

Rommel's advantage in the Western Desert was given by the mobile, mechanised Afrika Korps, which he used as a 'chase corps' to outmanoeuvre and defeat the enemy. British X Corps was Montgomery's 'corps de chasse' at Alamein, the first time this was used by the Eighth Army in the Western Desert.

out of the line, minus the 24th Armoured Brigade temporarily attached to the 1st Armoured Division, to reorganise for the 'big push' that was to follow the 9th Australian Division's attack to the north. It was hoped that Rommel would have committed his last reserves and have them eventually depleted, thus unable to face the final offensive intended to lead to the decisive breakout. This move was to be followed by the withdrawal of the 2nd New Zealand Division, and the possible redeployment of the 7th Armoured Division from the south, to provide the Eighth Army with a new 'corps de chasse' for, at least, the day of 28 October.

On the night of 25 October both 8th and 9th Armoured brigades pulled out of the line, withdrawing some 6 miles (10km) behind the front to reorganise and re-equip. Two days later, as dusk fell on 27 October, the 2nd New Zealand Division withdrew itself, being replaced in the line by the 1st South African Brigade, to rest and reorganise for the forthcoming offensive. On 26 October the 15th Panzer Division reported no losses amongst its own tanks while claiming the destruction of thirty-six enemy tanks, and the lack of any major activity on the enemy side suggested that the British armour had now reached their objectives. If the Axis forces thought that meant that no further action was to be taken by them, events soon proved how wrong this evaluation had been. By then the British frontline roughly matched the objectives given by the Oxalic Line, and faced to its westernmost prong a terrain feature known as 'Kidney Ridge' given its shape. To the south-west and north-west of it were two enemy positions known as Snipe and Woodcock, both lying less than 2 miles (3km) away from the frontline. These became the objective of another attack, which aimed to seize both during the night using 51st Infantry Division's units. They were to be joined at dawn by the advancing armour of the 1st Armoured Division, with the aim of provoking an enemy counterattack by a series of attempts to 'push on'. Confusion about orientation, given problems with map reading and the lack of clearly recognisable terrain features, spelt chaos amongst the attacking units with the headquarters of the two divisions estimating the positions of their targets with no less than 1.5km of difference. The attack started at 11pm on 26 October, with the two battalions of the 7th Motor Brigade moving toward Woodcock and those of the 2nd Rifle Brigade moving against Snipe (the former eventually joined by 133rd Lorried Brigade),

34. 'For you the war is over', a smiling 'Tommy' guarding Afrika Korps' prisoners of war.

both covered by the artillery fire of all the guns available to the XXX and X corps. Moving at night and facing some opposition from the enemy, the leading battalion of 7th Motor Brigade, the 2nd King's Royal Rifle Corps, failed to reach Woodcock and, at dawn, found itself to the south of it in an untenable position; its commander gave orders to move and eventually the battalion dug in just to the south-east of Point 33, away from its objective. To the south, 2nd Rifle Brigade used artillery fire as a guide, unaware of the fact that this had shifted north; after a march of 1.8 miles (3km), facing little opposition, the commander thought Snipe had been reached and ordered to dig in.

At about 6am on 27 October the 27th and 2nd Armoured brigades started their own advance toward Snipe and Woodcock respectively, facing an unexpected enemy reaction. Unknown to them, the previous evening the headquarters of 15th Panzer Division had ordered to counterattack the enemy positions using the available units, including those of the 21st Panzer Division and elements of the Italian Littorio and Ariete divisions. A misunderstanding of the situation and a certain amount of confusion about the actual position of the enemy forces also reigned amongst the Axis forces moving toward both objectives, with the fatal consequence that many German and Italian tanks fell victim to the British 6 pounder anti-tank guns; eventually a main counterattack was started at 4pm against Snipe, led by the units of the 21st Panzer Division. Once again, the German Panzers were to experience the uneasiness of an armoured counterattack running against well-hidden and highly effective anti-tank guns, this time manned by the men of 2nd Rifle Brigade. The crucial moment came at 5.30pm, when a group of fifteen Panzer III tanks approached the British positions from where three 6 pounder guns fired, hitting and destroying the three leading tanks. Those left eventually withdrew, only to seek cover and keep the British positions under fire until dark. For the valour demonstrated during that day, Lieutenant Colonel V.B. Turner of the Rifle Brigade was awarded the Victoria Cross. On their side, the Germans could only lick their wounds; on 27 October 15th Panzer Division claimed the destruction of some thirty-two enemy tanks and armoured fighting vehicles, which led to a total claim of 233 enemy tanks and AFVs destroyed between 23 and 28 October. Far less successful was the 21st Panzer, which claimed only twenty-four enemy tanks destroyed between 27 and 28 October; despite this, ultimately their own losses had been high. Too high, in fact, for they fell mostly on the vital anti-tank guns and armour: by 28 October the 15th Panzer was left with eight 50mm and one 76.2mm self-propelled guns in its anti-tank battalion, plus only twenty-four Panzers, which included three light Panzer IIs, and only eight long-barrelled Panzer IIIs and three Panzer IVs. On 29 October the 21st Panzer was still left with nineteen Panzer IIs, fifty-three short-barrelled and forty-three long-barrelled Panzer IIIs, and seven short-barrelled and fifteen long-barrelled Panzer IVs. As the Germans gave up their counterattack, on 28–29 October the lines were consolidated on both sides with the infantry digging in, and the activity being mainly reduced to artillery fire and small-scale attacks and patrols by infantry and tanks.

35. *The standard German anti-tank weapon in North Africa was the 50mm gun, here towed by a light half-tracked tractor.*

9th Australian Division Fight in the North

The battle is fought at Point 29 and at Woodcock and Snipe.

27 October		
	6am	British armour starts to advance on Woodcock and Snipe
	7.45am	90th 'Africa' Division is ordered to counterattack Point 29, held by the 9th Australian Division
	3.30pm	90th 'Africa' Division counterattacks Point 29
	4pm	German 21st Panzer Division's counterattack against Woodcock and Snipe
	5.15pm	90th 'Africa' Division incorrectly reports to have seized Point 29, the attack is called off
	5.30pm	The German counterattack reaches its peak, and is called off shortly thereafter

The first stage of 9th Australian Division's 'crumbling operation' to the north started with a stroke of luck, for a change; at dusk on 25 October a German reconnaissance party was captured, including one acting regimental and one acting battalion commander of the units deployed in the target area, both carrying detailed maps showing minefields and the tracks used by the Germans to move through them. The Australian attack started at midnight on the 25th, with an impressive artillery barrage that saw a total of 14,508 25 pounder shells and 1,066 of 5.5in. medium guns fired against the German positions. The leading companies of 26th Brigade suffered heavy casualties from German defence fire, eventually reaching their objective: Point 29, a small feature that provided excellent survey of the ground. At that point, before the artillery barrage lifted forward, ten carriers jumped forward carrying two infantry platoons and towing anti-tank guns; thanks to the captured maps, they were able to cover more than a kilometre distance to Point 29 in just 9 minutes, jumping out of the carriers close to it and attacking the stunned German defenders. While the fight for Point 29 started, the rest of the brigade moved onwards and, in spite of heavy German defences, eventually seized the surrounding area. At dawn, 26 October, the Australian infantry had dug into the new positions, waiting for the inevitable German counterattack.

Rommel's reaction to the Australian seizure of Point 29 can be viewed as a turning point in the battle: at 2.30pm on the 26th, the 90th Light 'Africa' Division, deployed north-west of Sidi Abd el-Rahman close to the sea, was committed and ordered to redeploy in the northern area. This was followed by another order coming at 7.45am on 27 October: the division was to attack Point 29 and seize it at once. A combat group formed around an infantry regiment did attack, with heavy artillery support, at 3.30pm on the 27th, but the dust and smoke soon generated the familiar chaos and confusion of the desert battles. At 5.15pm the combat group commander reported that Point 29 had been seized with heavy losses, which was only partially true since heavy losses had been suffered, but Point 29 had not been seized as a following report sadly communicated.

36. A Crusader and a Lee/Grant tank moving in the desert; tank formations could be easily spotted because of the thick clouds of sand they raised.

A new attack was organised for the following morning, and it started at 9am on 28 October, only to face the same heavy fire from the Australians, causing heavy losses. This, too, was called off by 12.30, with the Germans having only pushed a few hundred metres away from their objective, and the 90th Division was ordered to secure positions around Point 29 to prevent an enemy breakout. Heavy artillery fire, from both sides, fell on and around Point 29 throughout the day. That same night, 9th Australian Division attacked again with the aim of broadening the bridgehead in the northern area, and creating a suitable basis for the major attack towards the coast that was to follow. Under the support of what the Germans described as 'the heaviest artillery fire which had so far been experienced', the 20th Australian Brigade (along with 40th Royal Tank Regiment) on the left and 26th Brigade (with 46th Royal Tank Regiment) on the right, launched a two-pronged attack to the north and the north-east of Point 29, with the aim of severing the road and railroad communication lines running parallel to the coast. The attack, started at 10pm on 28 October, saw the 20th Brigade run into heavy enemy defences, losing contact with the supporting armour and eventually digging in about 800 metres north of Point 29; to its right, the 26th Brigade advanced north, eventually reaching the railway and the road, but heavy reaction from the German 90th Division, and the loss of communication, soon brought the decision to pull back.

The Australian attack, although falling short of its objectives, proved to be somewhat decisive; while another regiment from 90th Division attacked Point 29 from the west at 3.30pm on 29 October, without making progress and calling the attack off two hours later, in that same evening Rommel committed his last reserves. The 21st Panzer was to be moved north to act as a mobile reserve, its positions being relieved by the Italian Trieste Division, his last mobile reserve. To make sure Rommel had taken the bait, a new attack was launched by the 26th Australian Brigade at 10pm on 30 October, once more with the aim of reaching the railway and the road, swinging east following them

37. A German defence pit (in fact a hole dug in the sand) with a heavy, tripod mounted MG34 machine gun.

while also attacking north to the sea. The first stage of the plan saw the Australians advance deeply into the enemy lines, but the battalions were unable either to mop up the area or to keep in touch with one another; positions astride the railway and the road were secured, but the last phase of the attack – the drive to the sea, was checked at its very start by stubborn enemy resistance. For the role he played during this action, Sergeant W.H. Kibby was awarded a posthumous Victoria Cross, the second to be won by the Australians during the battle. At 7am on 31 October Rommel appeared at the headquarters of the 90th Division, ordering to counterattack the enemy positions between the railroad and the coast; a combat group of the division, supported by two others of both the 15th and the 21st Panzer divisions (the latter committing the bulk of its armour and anti-tank guns), launched the counterattack at 11am and eventually managed to establish contact with the elements of the 90th Division (now squeezed between the Australian positions astride the railroad and those on the east) by 1.25pm, but was unable to dislodge the 26th Australian Brigade from its positions.

At dusk both sides were exhausted, and the harshness of the fight is clearly portrayed in this account:

> The first light of dawn revealed a sight that was none too good for chaps with weak stomachs. Dead and mutilated bodies were to be seen wherever one looked, together with burnt out guns, tanks and weapons of all description.
>
> from Barr, *Pendulum of War*, p.379

Nevertheless, both sides had reasons to be satisfied; the Germans had somehow re-established the line and prevented a major crisis in the north; the Australians had achieved their goal of distracting Rommel's attention from the main area and had forced him to commit his last reserves. However, 90th Division was left with no clear orders for the next day, but at this point the Eighth Army was just about to start the last phase of the offensive: it was to be decisive.

Operation Supercharge

Plans for Supercharge; the battle is fought in the north

28 October		
8am	Montgomery holds a conference to discuss the further plans, which leads to the Supercharge plan
9am	90th 'Africa' Division again counterattacks Point 29, facing heavy opposition from the Australians
12.30	90th 'Africa' Division's attack is called off, having not reached Point 29
10pm	9th Australian Division, with armour support, attacks north, toward the coast

29 Oct		Battle in the north between Germans and Australians
	3.30pm	New attack against Point 29 by the 90th 'Africa' Division, it is called off two hours later
30 Oct		New Australian attack in the north
	10pm	New attack north by the 9th Australian Division, leading across the railway running parallel to the coast
		German counterattack against the Australian drive to the coast
31 Oct	**7am**	Rommel reaches the HQ of 90th 'Africa' Division and orders to counterattack the Australian units astride the railway
	11am	The German counterattack commences
	1.25pm	Advancing German units re-establish a frontline, but are unable to dislodge the Australians from their positions

At 8am on 28 October, General Montgomery held a conference to analyse the further development of Eighth Army's battle plans; for the moment, the offensive was closed down on the entire front with the exception of the 9th Australian Division's attack in the north. Recognising that the entire Panzer Army Africa was now fully deployed along the whole front, Montgomery came to the conclusion that no breakout was possible from the positions running along the Oxalic Line. To prepare for the decisive blow, he ordered 1st Armoured Division to be withdrawn from the front, its place being temporarily taken by the 10th Armoured Division until this too was to be pulled off in the evening of 29 October. The new thrust was in fact aimed at the same Skinflint objective of the earlier Lightfoot plan, which was the Sidi Rahman track running from north to south, right behind the positions of the Oxalic Line; this time, however, Montgomery had to face the serious problem of a shortage of fresh troops with which the new offensive could be conducted. Acknowledging that General Freyberg, the commander of 2nd New Zealand Division, was his best divisional

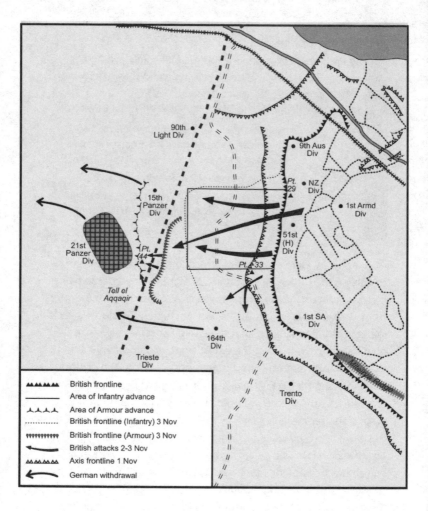

British frontline
Area of Infantry advance
Area of Armour advance
British frontline (Infantry) 3 Nov
British frontline (Armour) 3 Nov
British attacks 2-3 Nov
Axis frontline 1 Nov
German withdrawal

commander, Montgomery wanted his division to be in the lead, even though the actual condition of his fighting units was far from ideal. Since the start of Lightfoot, the 2nd New Zealand Division had suffered some 900 casualties, almost entirely coming from the infantry units and mainly amongst the fighting soldiers 'who carry rifle and the Bren gun', as General Freyberg described to General Leese on 27 October. Thus, out of a total strength of 11,774 men the division could still muster only an average strength in its six infantry battalions of some 500 men, which meant – having subtracted the 340-odd men in headquarters and support companies – that an average fighting strength of only 200 men (i.e. fifty per company) would have in reality been available. This was in fact the average fighting strength of most of the infantry units which had been fighting hard during the last days, and the only possible reassurance came from the certainty that on the other side the situation was no better.

Rommel was, like Montgomery, facing a potential crisis: at the end of October the situation of his army had not improved at all, given both the lack of supplies and reinforcements. Shortage of ammunition was a sore point, in this case more than the lack of fuel. In light of the scarce supplies received by the Panzer Army, by 1 November 1942 it was reckoned that it was no longer possible to fight effectively any major enemy offensive, and that units had to restrain themselves to fight only at the level of strong reconnaissance patrols or if any concentration of enemy forces was actually spotted. Reinforcements were limited to only two Italian infantry battalions, hardly matching the losses suffered by the Italian units, not to mention the German ones, and the only German reinforcement scheduled to arrive was a battalion of Nebelwerfer (rocket launchers) which was not expected to appear before 10 November. A detailed comparison of the armour situation on both sides reveals the actual strength available. By 1 November the Panzer Army Africa still had in its two Panzer divisions ninety modern tanks (the long-barrelled Panzer III and IV variants – those really effective against the

38. The Universal, or Bren Carrier, was the most widely used infantry tracked vehicle in the British Army.

Eighth Army's armour), out of a total of 192 tanks, distributed as follows: fifty-five with the 15th Panzer Division (five light Panzer IIs, fifteen old Panzer IIIs and three Panzer IVs, plus twenty-seven new long-barrelled Panzer IIIs and five Panzer IVs), plus another 137 with the 21st Panzer Division (nineteen light Panzer IIs, fifty-three old Panzer IIIs and seven Panzer IVs, forty-three new long-barrelled Panzer IIIs and fifteen Panzer IVs). There were also some 189 Italian medium tanks, thirty-eight with the Littorio and 124 with the Ariete armoured divisions, plus some other twenty-seven with the Trieste Motorised Division. The Eighth Army had, apart from Valentine and Stuart tanks, around 487 modern and effective tanks (the total was about 700) mostly with the 1st Armoured Division, since the 10th Armoured had lent its 8th Armoured Brigade to it and, with the 24th Armoured Brigade still greatly understrength given the losses suffered during Lightfoot, was in practice no longer fit for frontline duty. Thus the 1st Armoured had in its 2nd and 8th Armoured Brigades some thirty-nine M3 Lee/Grants, 113 M4 Shermans, forty-six Crusader IIIs and seventy-three Crusader II tanks, while the 9th Armoured Brigade attached to the 2nd New Zealand Division mustered some forty Lee/Grants, thirty-nine Shermans, twenty-four Crusader IIs and twenty-nine Crusader III tanks. The 7th Armoured Division, held in reserve with its 22nd Armoured Brigade, also added some other fifty-four Lee/Grants, ten Crusader IIIs and twenty Crusader II tanks.

All in all, the battle about to be fought was somewhat of a 'narrow margin' for both sides. Both Rommel and Montgomery had chances for success, but any serious mistake on their side might easily turn into a critical situation from which any recovery was impossible. Montgomery had, of course, some advantages over his adversary; first of all the availability of virtually unlimited supplies, which enabled him to use the tremendous artillery firepower of the Eighth Army almost at will, and also the crisis the Germans were facing in a critical sector: their anti-tank guns. By 31 October the 15th Panzer Division only had some thirty-eight 50mm and 76.2mm guns left in its units, having lost thirty-two of them during the first week of fighting and also having roughly twenty-one under short- and long-term repair. No matter what, this was a 'one-shot' chance of blunting the armoured edge of the Eighth Army; if this failed, there was no way back.

Operation Supercharge was a kind of carbon copy of Operation Lightfoot, with a few differences; the availability of artillery would allow counterbattery fire as well as a barrage against the enemy defences. Additionally, there would not be any elaborate or deep mine defence to break through, only scattered mine patches which, although troublesome, were no real hurdle. The attack was to be delivered on a front approximately 2.5 miles (4km) wide, running from Point 29 down to Woodcock in the south. The 151st and 152nd British Infantry brigades (from 50th and 51st Infantry divisions), both attached to the 2nd New Zealand Division, were to take the lead, each one supported by a Valentine tank battalion. The objective of infantry units was a line some 5km from the starting point (approximately 3.5km behind the Axis defences); 9th Armoured Brigade was to follow up and advance for a further 2km, reaching the Rahman track which was to be crossed alongside the units of the 1st Armoured Division. Once in position a battle was to be fought with the Axis armour in the open, with the aim of defeating them once and for all.

Tell el Aqqaqir

1 Nov

Start of Operation Supercharge

9.15pm	RAF bombers attack enemy positions at Tell el Aqqaqir

2 November

Supercharge, battle at Tell el Aqqaqir

1.05am	Eighth Army's artillery attacks enemy positions, shortly afterwards the infantry starts to advance
3.44am	Advancing infantry reports reaching the objectives
4.15am	15th and 21st Panzer divisions ordered to counterattack
4.45am	Panzer Army Africa reports that most of the units at the front have been overrun
6.15am	British armour starts to advance through the paths cleared by the infantry, attacking Tell el Aqqaqir
7am	British 1st Armoured Division starts to deploy in the conquered ground in front of Tell el Aqqaqir
7.10am	3rd Hussars suffer heavy losses from 15th Panzer Division attacks
8.15am	After a report by Afrika Korps' commander, General von Thoma, Rommel decides to start a step by step withdrawal to positions at Fuka
12.40	German 15th and 21st Panzer divisions counterattack with all available tanks
c.1pm	15th Panzer Division reports one battalion to have only five serviceable tanks left, the counterattack is called off some time later in early afternoon
Night	51st Division captures Skinflint and Snipe positions

The Battlefield: What Actually Happened?

Axis withdrawal from El Alamein starts

3 November	**1.15am**	The British 1st Armoured Division attacks west, but it is quickly halted by enemy fire
	3am	The Axis units start to withdraw from the line, first the Italian X, XX and XXI corps and then the Afrika Korps
	10am	The Eighth Army notices the Axis withdrawal
	1.30pm	Rommel receives a message from Hitler forbidding any retreat, Axis units are ordered to stand fast on the positions they have actually reached
	4pm	5th Indian Brigade moves west to attack the enemy lines
	5.45pm	New attack by British 1st Armoured Division to the west, held up by German rearguards

39. *Infantry advancing along with Valentine tanks; the second battle of Alamein was the first real attempt at infantry–tanks cooperation.*

40. A Crusader tank damaged and abandoned.

ROMMEL'S LACK OF SUPPLIES

In September 1942 Hitler promised Rommel some reinforcements, including the heavy Tiger tanks and the Nebelwerfer rocket launcher. These, officially called 'smoke throwers' to hide their purpose, were multi-barrelled rocket projectors used to replace the artillery, very effective but also scarcely precise.

The Battlefield: What Actually Happened?

At 9.15pm on 1 November more than eighty RAF bombers dropped their bombs on targets in the Rahman track area, around the key position of Tell el Aqqaqir. At 1.05am on 2 November the attack started with another deluge of fire from Eighth Army's artillery falling both on the Axis artillery and on the forward defence positions, delivering some 150,000 shells into an area of about 4km^2. Immediately after the barrage lifted forward, both brigades started to advance and met little opposition from the enemy. Several German and Italian prisoners were taken with few losses on their own side, but confusion, generated by smoke and dust, reigned again, resulting in a splitting up of the leading companies. Nevertheless, at 3.44am infantry reported that it had reached its objective line on time, which was quite a remarkable achievement. With the engineers clearing five lanes across scattered minefields, the tanks were able to follow up closely, even though 9th Armoured Brigade lost more than forty tanks due to mechanical breakdowns during the approach march from the El Alamein station, leaving only some ninety-four still fit for action. With a delay of half an hour, at 6.15am on 2 November the British armour started to advance across the paths seized by the infantry and cleared by the engineers to their objective: the Rahman track, which they approached before dawn.

Already at midnight on 2 November, the air bombardment suggested a new offensive was about to start and the headquarters of Panzer Army Africa issued its own order: all the positions were to be held no matter what, not an inch of terrain was to be surrendered without a hard fight. In reality it was another matter entirely; heavily hit by the artillery barrage and overwhelmed by the two advancing brigades, units on the frontline fell one after another; one battalion of 90th Light Division in the north, along with another one of 15th Panzer Division in the south, were soon overrun and at 4.45am it was reported that only one Italian 'Bersaglieri' infantry battalion (sharpshooters) was still holding the line, soon to be overrun. Half an hour earlier, following reports of an enemy armoured breakthrough on the Rahman track, both 15th and 21st Panzer divisions were ordered to counterattack. Even before the 9th Armoured Brigade started its march, elements from both German divisions, supported by Italian tanks, attacked the leading armour of 8th and 50th Royal Tank Regiments, supporting the advancing infantry brigades, each with about thirty-eight Valentines, and the armoured cars of the Royal Dragoon Guards that advanced to Tell el Aqqaqir. A little while later, the tanks of 9th Armoured Brigade arrived, immediately attacking the enemy positions along the Rahman track – which included some twenty-four of the deadly 88mm guns – with its three battalions deployed as follows from north to south: 3rd Hussars, Royal Wiltshire Yeomanry and Warwickshire Yeomanry, supported by the anti-tank guns of 14th Sherwood Foresters. Led by Major Michael Everleigh's B Squadron, the 3rd Hussars were the first to attack the enemy on the Rahman track, immediately destroying four enemy anti-tank guns; at that point the first light of the day had the silhouettes of the tanks standing clearly against the rising sun, immediately attracting the enemy fire. Everleigh's tank was put out of action, but he continued to issue orders walking from tank to tank; the rest of the battalion attacked the enemy anti-tank gun position until facing the advancing German tanks of 15th Panzer Division. By 7.10am, the 3rd Hussars were only left with seven tanks out of some forty, with four of its officers still alive and unwounded.

The Royal Wiltshire Yeomanry had better luck since it was able to storm the enemy anti-tank positions by surprise before dawn, only

El Alamein Victoria Crosses, part three

William Henry (Bill) Kibby, the last to win a VC at Alamein, was an Australian born in England who joined the army in 1936. A Sergeant in the 2/48th Battalion (26th Brigade), he distinguished himself at Miteirya Ridge on 23 October in leadership and bravery. On 30–31 October he attacked a German position alone, and was killed.

41. A Blenheim light bomber flying low over a British motorised column in the desert.

to be attacked at close range by 21st Panzer Division's tanks. A tank crew member vividly described the experience of tank combat:

> Flash, flash, flash… in a great semi-circle the guns of the enemy wink viciously back at him as great balls of fire seem to leap out of the sand and hurtle towards the oncoming tanks. Some miss their marks and bounce on the sand, to die out gracefully like fireworks in the sky. Others land with a sickening metallic clang on the Crusaders and explosions add dull thuds to the pandemonium of sounds that fills the shattered air.
>
> from Barr, *Pendulum of War*, p.387

To the south, the Lee/Grants and Shermans of the Warwickshire Yeomanry attacked the enemy positions on the Rahman track only to find themselves out in the open, lacking any kind of cover. Under a hail of fire, from both anti-tank guns and Panzer tanks, the British tanks initially laid a smokescreen but, as soon as this was removed by the wind, they found themselves under attack from three different positions and quickly lost most of their tanks. As recalled by a (lucky) crew member of the C Squadron:

Tanks were brewing up all round us but we didn't get hit. There were flashes from guns on all sides and it wasn't until the sun came up that we knew which direction we were facing. We picked up two survivors from a 1st Troop tank and dropped them off by a gunpit near another tank. Then the Colonel came on the air: 'For God's sake get those bloody guns before they get the lot of us!'

From Perrett, *Iron Fist. Classic Armoured Warfare*, pp.94–5

Eventually only seven tanks of the Warwickshires were able to join the Royal Wiltshires. At about 7am the leading elements of 2nd Armoured Brigade started to reach the 9th Brigade on the Rahman track. The latter paid a very high price for its outstanding achievement: thirty-one officers and 198 other ranks were either killed, wounded or missing and, when the brigade eventually withdrew in the evening, it had lost seventy tanks out of ninety-four. Around 7am the 1st Armoured Division started to deploy in the conquered ground: 2nd Armoured Brigade was sent to a position 1.8 miles (3km) north-west of Tell el Aqqaqir, the 8th Armoured Brigade to take position on Tell el Aqqaqir and the 7th Motor Brigade to deploy between them. Soon the two armoured brigades ran themselves into a chaotic situation in the area, further aggravated by reduced visibility due to the smoke and dust raised by the battle being fought; paths were crossed, the 8th Brigade was told to make ground to the south-west of the 2nd, and both brigades were soon under the enemy anti-tank guns' fire. Eventually both took position east of the track, after the loss of fifty-four tanks (forty of which were only damaged), and started to fire on the enemy. At 12.40 the Germans counterattacked with all their available tanks, leading to the greatest tank battle fought at El Alamein; less than half an hour later 15th Panzer Division reported how, in spite of the claimed destruction of some sixty enemy tanks, one of its battalions was down to five serviceable Panzer tanks and that the regimental commander was dead. In fact,

THE BERSAGLIERI

The Bersaglieri (literally sharpshooters) are one of the elite units of the Italian infantry, traditionally the highly mobile one which, in the Western Desert, provided the only motorised (either with motorcycles or truck borne) Italian infantry units. Their feathered headgear, helmets included, are a peculiar characteristic.

42. Tanks burning in front of the wire marking Rommel's 'devil's garden' mined boxes on the Alamein defence line.

the British anti-tank and tank guns' fire produced the same effects already experienced by British armour against the German defences in the Western Desert campaign; losses were high on both sides, the 1st Armoured Division did not penetrate the enemy defences, but the Axis forces were destroyed one by one. Finally, early in the afternoon, the Germans started to call their attacks off.

The Breakout

The breakthrough

<table>
<tr><td rowspan="10">4 November</td></tr>
<tr><td>2.15am</td><td>Rommel orders the temporary commander of the Afrika Korps, Colonel Bayerlein, to start a major withdrawal west</td></tr>
<tr><td>2.30am</td><td>Allied artillery bombardment on all known enemy positions; 5th Indian Brigade attacks south of Tell el Aqqaqir</td></tr>
<tr><td>6.15am</td><td>Argyll and Sutherland Highlanders attack Tell el Aqqaqir</td></tr>
<tr><td>6.45am</td><td>Tell el Aqqaqir is seized by units of British 51st Infantry Division, British units start pursuing the retreating Germans and attack the Italian Ariete Armoured Division</td></tr>
<tr><td>2.45pm</td><td>News of the British attack against the Ariete Division reach Rommel's HQ</td></tr>
<tr><td>3pm</td><td>Rommel gives the definitive order for all units to withdraw west, to Fuka, under the cover of darkness</td></tr>
<tr><td>3.30pm</td><td>The Italian Ariete Division, attacked from the north and the south, is eventually destroyed by the British armoured units, leaving no major Axis unit to face Eighth Army's advance</td></tr>
<tr><td>8.50pm</td><td>Hitler agrees to the withdrawal, but his message is received by Rommel only the following morning</td></tr>
</table>

General von Vaerst had good reasons to be proud of his men, for during 2 November they claimed the destruction of at least sixty enemy tanks and successfully managed to prevent their breakthrough. But he knew this victory was a double-edged sword; his division was bleeding white, and at the end of the day it was left with only nine running tanks and six 50mm anti-tank guns. Additionally, 21st Panzer Division was down to twenty operational Panzer III and IV tanks. With the loss of the bulk of one of its infantry regiments, the division could only rely on its artillery to push the enemy back. And this was not an isolated case; as the sun fell over the battlefield, Rommel was to discover that he only had thirty-eight German tanks and twenty-four of the 88mm guns, his most effective weapon against the enemy armour. This was the moment for decisive action; after the report made at 8.15am on 2 November by the Afrika Korps commander, General von Thoma, Rommel decided that the only way to prevent an enemy breakthrough was to start a step by step withdrawal to the positions at Fuka – some 43–50 miles (70–80km) west of El Alamein. The Italian Ariete Division was to deploy at Tell el Aqqaqir, covering the retreat of the remnants of the Italian infantry (XXI Corps), with the remnants of the Italian armour (XX Corps) deploying to the left. In the south, the Italian X Corps, greatly lacking motor transport, was to start its withdrawal west that same night, covering some 12–15km. Eventually, the remnants of his mobile forces – including the Italian XX Corps, the Afrika Korps with the two Panzer divisions, plus the 90th and 164th light divisions – were to create a screen to slow down the enemy advance; their withdrawal was to start early on 3 November, so that by the same evening a defence line could be established approximately 8km to the west of the Rahman track.

Withdrawals started as planned at 3am on 3 November, first with the Italian units of X Corps, along with the German Ramcke Brigade, pulling back from the south, followed by the 90th Light Division in the north and by both Italian XX and XXI corps, that started to redeploy to the south of Tell el Aqqaqir, the first step of a movement that was to lead them back to Fuka. Only the 164th Light Division was delayed, mainly because of the sheer lack of motor transport. At 1.30pm Rommel received a message from Hitler's headquarters clearly stating that the Panzer Army was 'not to yield a step', but was rather to fight on its positions. Facing a difficult situation, and pressed by General von Thoma, Rommel was not able to do anything other than seek for a compromise solution; since the units could not get back to their positions, he ordered the bulk of infantry – the Italian X and XXI corps plus the 90th Light Division – to stand fast where they were, while the

Afrika Korps was to withdraw some 5 miles (8km) west of Tell el Aqqaqir soon followed by the Italian armour of the XX Corps.

During the night of 2 November, the British 51st Division attacked to the south of 2nd New Zealand Division's bridgehead, with the aim of capturing both the Skinflint and Snipe positions, both taken quite easily during that very night. Meanwhile, a new plan was devised for the 1st Armoured Division: following the advance of 7th Motor Brigade on the Rahman track, to start that same night, 2nd and 8th Armoured Brigades were to advance in line pushing some 5km behind the enemy lines which, once broken through, would have been crossed by the 7th Armoured Division spearheading the advance toward Fuka. At 1.15am on 3 November the three battalions of 7th Motor Brigade started their attack, soon to be halted by the enemy fire. Such a failure led to a change of plans for both armoured brigades, now intended to fight their way through the enemy defences. Their attack started at 5.45pm on 3 November, while the Axis forces were already withdrawing, but soon ran into troubles; to the north the 2nd Armoured Brigade was held up by the rearguards of the two Panzer divisions and of the Italian Littorio Division, while to the south the 8th Brigade ran into the defences of two anti-tank battalions that spread havoc with their deadly, and unexpected, fire. By the end of the day both brigades had lost around twenty-six tanks, without reaching the Rahman track. However, time was

GUSTAV VON VAERST

A career officer who fought in the First World War, in 1939 he was commander of an infantry brigade of a Panzer division. In 1939–41 he fought in all the 'Blitzkrieg' campaigns until becoming, in December 1941, commander of the 15th Panzer Division. Made commander of German 5th Panzer Army in Tunisia, he became a prisoner in May 1943.

43. German General von Thoma, the commander of the Afrika Korps, took over command of the German rearguards during the last stage of Operation Supercharge; after his capture, he was brought to General Montgomery.

running out for Rommel; having noticed the enemy withdrawal at about 10am on 3 November, around noon Montgomery issued new orders for the following day instructing the 51st Division to attack and seize the Rahman track and Tell el Aqqaqir, only to issue new orders following reports of a general retreat on the side of the Panzer Army Africa. These instructed the British X Corps to strike north to the coast road, while the New Zealand Division, reinforced, was to strike west with the aim of driving towards Fuka and, if necessary, toward Mersa Matruh.

Already at 4pm on 3 November, facing the enemy withdrawal, the 5th Indian Brigade started moving to attack the enemy forces to the south-west of Tell el Aqqaqir, only to be delayed by a 12-mile (20km) march across the desert which required a 1-hour postponement of the artillery bombardment that was to open the path for the last assault. The bombardment finally started at 2.30am on 4 November,

44. An infantry squad in the desert, all wearing the khaki drill shirts and shorts. Armament includes the .303 Lee Enfield rifle and the Bren light machine gun.

hitting hard all the known enemy positions. Immediately followed were attacks by 5th Indian Brigade south of Tell el Aqqaqir; the position itself was attacked at 6.15am by the Argyll and Sutherland Highlanders of 154th Infantry Brigade. Neither force faced any serious opposition from the enemy, which had apparently simply melted away, and at 6.45am Point 45, better known as Tell el Aqqaqir, finally fell into the hands of the Eighth Army. At this point it was clear that Rommel's forces were withdrawing, but not everywhere. At dawn the British 1st Armoured Division moved, its 2nd Armoured Brigade in the lead, hoping to start a free chase of the withdrawing enemy forces; however, it soon ran head-on into the rearguards of the Afrika Korps, led by General von Thoma who personally took over command of its 'combat detachment'. This small force, equipped with both anti-tank guns and tanks, checked 2nd Armoured Brigade's advance throughout the morning. Eventually, the 'combat detachment' was destroyed shortly before noon, and von Thoma surrendered to Captain Grant Singer of the 10th Hussars. A better fate was met by the 7th Armoured Division, which advanced right into a gap between the remnants of the Italian Trento and Bologna divisions of the XXI Corps in the north, and managed to envelope the armoured Ariete Division from the south; by 3.30pm the Ariete was attacked from the north too, thus completing its encirclement.

With his forces halted before the planned withdrawal had been completed, Rommel had the bulk of the Panzer Army Africa – which were the infantry units, mostly lacking motor transport, while the two Panzer divisions still could manage to break away from the fight – exposed out in the open, and the consequences were now dramatically clear; Eighth Army's advance was threatening to destroy whatever was still left of the Panzer Army in spite of Hitler's 'stand fast' order. It was only after Field Marshal Albert Kesselring, the German Air Force commander in the Mediterranean, offered him his own support against Hitler's order that Rommel would take the chance of disobeying it (although, in the meantime, he asked for a free hand in his morning report to him). Eventually, between 2am and 2.15am on 4 November Rommel told Colonel Fritz Bayerlein, temporary commander of the Afrika Korps, to start a major withdrawal of his units to the west, if necessary pulling back approximately 12 miles (20km). There was not to be any unnecessary last stand on the actual positions, no unnecessary casualties of a battle already lost. News of the destruction on the field of the Ariete Division reached Rommel's headquarters at 2.45pm, clearing the picture: there was practically nothing left to halt the British armour advancing toward the coastal road. Shortly after 3pm Rommel gave the final order: every unit was to retreat west, taking advantage of darkness, to the positions at Fuka. At 8.50pm the same day Hitler belatedly agreed to authorise the retreat, an order Rommel did not receive until the morning after. The second battle of El Alamein was now over.

Eighth Army's pursuit of the remnants of the Panzer Army Africa started early on 5 November, when a first summary of the battle

ROMMEL'S 'COMBAT DETACHMENT'

The 'Kampfstaffel' (combat detachment) was a battalion-sized combat unit with a varying composition and organisation, often equipped with a variety of captured enemy vehicles and armour. Put directly at Rommel's disposal, it was used by him (sometimes first hand) to face any impromptu situation or need on the battlefield.

which had just ended was already possible; by then a total of 2,922 German and 4,184 Italian soldiers had been taken prisoner, with a series of estimates of 1,149 German soldiers killed, 3,866 wounded and 8,050 missing or captured, plus some other 971 Italian soldiers dead, 933 wounded and 15,522 missing or captured. Only by 11 November did more complete figures emerge after the remnants of the Axis forces had been rounded up; by then there were some 30,000 prisoners which included 7,802 Germans and 22,071 Italians. Exact figures concerning the Axis losses at Second Alamein are hardly available; of the Italian units only the remnants of the Trieste Division, with a few stragglers from other units, managed to retreat along with the Germans; all other Italian divisions (the infantry Pavia, Bologna, Brescia, Trento, the armoured Ariete and Littorio and the Folgore paratrooper division) were unable to, and therefore were completely destroyed. No German units were completely destroyed, although they all were badly mauled and by 18 November Afrika Korps' total strength was less than 18,000 – which is more than 30,000 fewer than before the battle started on 23 October. Overall losses can be estimated at about 9,000 killed and missing in action, 15,000 wounded and 35,000 prisoners for all the Axis forces. This was without taking into account the huge losses of tanks, guns, weapons and equipment. Eighth Army's losses were in no way inferior to these; 2,350 men killed in action, plus some other 2,260

45. *Bayonets fixed, Eighth Army's soldiers capture the crew of a German Panzer III tank in the desert.*

missing, and another 8,950 wounded. Tank losses stood at 332 British tanks, against claims for 259 enemy tanks, and 111 guns (against claims for 254 enemy guns) destroyed, although some of the tanks were actually recovered and repaired. Montgomery came close to his aim to 'destroy Rommel and his Army.' However, in the end, it was a goal he fell short of.

AFTER THE BATTLE

The Pursuit

By 5 November the remnants of the Panzer Army Africa reached the position at Fuka, some 31 miles (50km) behind the positions they evacuated during the night. The Eighth Army started its own pursuit, with the 1st Armoured Division in the lead, soon followed by the 2nd New Zealand Division (the only one actually motorised, since the others needed to be provided with a motor transport pool) moving to the south of the coast road, and the 7th and 10th Armoured divisions following up. On the night between 5 and 6 November the 1st Armoured Division managed to break through the positions held by the German 15th and 21st Panzer divisions, and Rommel ordered his units to withdraw back to the Mersa Matruh position, some 40 miles (65km) further west. The Panzer Army stood there on 7 November, when an order from Mussolini told Rommel that no withdrawal west of the Libyan–Egyptian frontier would be allowed. Having already disobeyed Hitler's orders, Rommel easily replied that because of the losses, in particular amongst the Italian forces, no stand there was possible. Two days later Mussolini gave him a free hand. Unknown to Rommel, the Eighth Army's advance came short of its objectives for one very simple reason: after the long battle, unprepared for these fast movements, advancing units ran out of fuel and were forced to halt. The following night the bulk of Panzer Army Africa simply slipped away from the Mersa Matruh position, to continue its march to the west that led it to reach Sidi Barrani at first and then, after being forced to evacuate it by the spearheads of the Eighth Army on the evening of 9 November, to the position of Sollum and the Halfaya Pass, marking the Libyan–Egyptian frontier.

Now marching at full speed, the spearheads of the Eighth Army held the advantage over their enemy; on 11 November units from the 2nd New Zealand Division and the 7th Armoured Division attacked Sollum and the Halfaya Pass, seized it taking some 600 Italian prisoners but found that the road going up on the escarpment had been demolished. Threatened by this successful move, Rommel's Panzer Army Africa withdrew at full speed to Bardia, quickly abandoning Egypt just four and a half months after its invasion. Now fully exposed in the Cyrenaica 'bulge', the same one that had already been fateful to the Italian Army two years before, Rommel decided to retreat west at full speed. By 13 November Tobruk had been evacuated and quickly seized by 7th Armoured Division, without a fight. For the next ten days Rommel's forces drove at full speed, marching to the all too familiar position of Mersa el Brega between Cyrenaica and Tripolitania, the same position where his own forces had started their first offensive in March–April 1941. On 14 November four columns, all under command of the 7th Armoured Division, were formed for the pursuit, each built around an armoured formation and with detachments of field, anti-tank, and anti-aircraft artillery plus engineers. Temporarily halted by the lack of fuel, Rommel's forces were almost caught by the advancing columns on 15 November, but managed to move west and took advantage of the heavy rain that fell on the following day, making any movement impossible. On the 18th one of the pursuing columns made contact with the rearguards of Rommel's army, but since he had received supplies the march westwards continued at full speed. On 20 November the Eighth Army entered Benghazi for the third time, but in spite of Montgomery's urges it was not

46. A destroyed Italian medium tank in the desert.

possible to prevent Rommel's forces from reaching the Mersa el Brega position on the night of 23–24 November.

The first part of the pursuit was now over, and one ought to remark how, at the end of it, the Eighth Army was facing the same conditions the Panzer Army Africa had faced before the Alamein battle: the supply dumps, used during the battle with generosity, were now nearly 621 miles (1,000km) behind the leading units of the Eighth Army. These were, just like the German and the Italian units, not at all in the best condition either to pursue or to attack the enemy without taking risks; the *c.*13,000 losses suffered by Eighth Army at El Alamein mainly fell amongst the frontline combat units, e.g. infantry battalions and companies and tank crews, and could not be replaced quickly, for one ought to remember the battle had only ended less than three weeks before. Montgomery was certainly cautious when he ordered to prepare stocks and reserves for a major attack against Mersa el Brega, but his desire to avoid any setback (or even defeat) can be understood. Only after a long pause were the 2nd New Zealand Division able to attack Rommel's defences at Mersa el Brega along with the 7th Armoured Division; the attack, started on the night of 14–15 December, was again only to face the rearguards of Panzer Army Africa. Threatened by the 2nd New Zealand's 'hook' to the south, Rommel ordered to withdraw west and by 19 December another position was built at Buerat, some 155 miles (250km) from Tripoli. Deaf to all the requests coming from Hitler and Mussolini, Rommel – who certainly identified the Allied landing of 8 November 1942 in the French North-West Africa as a serious threat – was completely willing to yield the terrain in the face of Eighth Army's possible onslaught. When its new attack against the Buerat line came on 15 January 1943, Rommel ordered a fresh withdrawal the following night. At this point it was only a matter of days; on 20 January the British 51st Division clashed with the 90th Light 'Africa' Division, which opened the way to Tripoli. The 11th Hussars entered the city, facing no opposition early on 23 January 1943, and by noon Montgomery received the formal surrender from the hands of the Italian vice-governor of Tripolitania. While, between 25 and 29 November, the German 90th Division checked the British advance at Zuara, the first Axis forces under Rommel's command crossed the Libyan–Tunisian border to establish their positions on the Mareth line. On 15 February 1943 the last rearguards of 15th Panzer Division crossed the border, thus putting an end to the Western Desert campaign.

THE LEGACY

El Alamein as a British Victory

On 15 November 1942 the church bells of Britain were rung to celebrate what Churchill described as 'the hinge of fate': the victory in North Africa that would have changed once and for all the destiny of the whole campaign. The fact that those bells had been silent since 1939, when the war broke out, gives a rough idea of how important this recent event was for both the leaders and the public. Since September 1939 Britain had faced alternating fortunes, first the defeat of the joint coalition with France and the 'miracle' of Dunkerque, which though rescuing a good deal of the British Army in the continent did not alter the fact that the same army had been defeated, then the threat of a German invasion and the air war started in the summer of 1940. Just like Dunkerque, the victory achieved in the Battle of Britain was not a full one; Britain had managed to push away the threat of a German invasion, but the fact that German aircraft were still bombing British cities even after the end of the battle largely contributed to make this look more like the enemy had been beaten but not defeated. This kind of feeling accompanied most of the British successes in the years to come; the defeat of the Italian forces both in the Western Desert and in East Africa in

1940–41 eventually turned into only temporary successes, since shortly afterwards the fortunes of war saw the Germans once again winning their own victories both in the Western Desert and in the Balkans. Since June 1941, after the German invasion of the Soviet Union, Britain no longer stood alone against Germany and the Axis, but that did not mean her fortunes improved at all.

By the end of 1941 it was all too clear how Churchill's 'blood, sweat and tears' had turned into a grim reality. Successes on the battlefield came, along with the new reality of the strategic air war against Germany, but these proved to be anything but decisive. Rommel's retreat from Cyrenaica in December 1941 meant that Operation Crusader ended with a British victory, but his subsequent drive into western Cyrenaica early in 1942 clearly suggested this had been just another temporary success. The situation even worsened following the entry of Japan into the war, and things deteriorated both in Europe and in the Western Desert during the spring and summer of 1942. Rommel's success at Tobruk and his invasion of Egypt brought the Axis threat directly against the vital core of the British-held Middle East. The failure that same August of the first, large-scale 'rehearsal' of the attempt to regain a foothold on the European continent, the Dieppe landing, openly suggested how – after three years of war and too much 'blood, sweat and tears' – the war was still to be hard fought, and yet to be won. The reality of the facts, with the benefit of hindsight, was certainly different than people may have seen at the time; Rommel's drive into Egypt was actually largely based on a bluff, and, to say the very least, it never really threatened the British positions in the Middle East, while even the Dieppe fiasco (no matter how costly) was just a premature attempt, and no real setback. But all this can be said with the advantage of hindsight; for the British people, living under the threat of the German bombing since the summer of 1940, facing the privation of food rationing and the danger of their loved ones fighting all around the world, the summer of 1942 looked like the prelude to a major disaster.

El Alamein's Place in History

The successes on the Alamein battlefield in July and September were, once again, kind of half-baked victories: Rommel's drive to Alexandria and the Nile had been blunted, but the fact that his army still stood there meant there was a threat, whether this was a real one or not. This is the real meaning of the victory at El Alamein in October–November 1942; for the very first time in years, this was not an uncertain, temporary success. This was a real victory, the first that Britain could claim against the Axis forces and, as Churchill and other leaders clearly imagined, probably the last, with the invasion of the French North-West Africa just four days after the victory at Alamein, the United States had finally entered into the war. After Alamein there would not be a British victory again, no matter how crucial or meaningful the British contribution had been. Thereafter there would only be Allied victories: Tunisia; the invasion of Sicily in July 1943; the invasion and the surrender of Italy the following September; the seizure of the first capital city of the Axis – Rome, in June 1944; shortly followed by the landings in Normandy and the beginning of the decisive campaign in North-West Europe. El Alamein was back then, as it still is today, one of the most important British victories during the Second World War, and as such a decisive victory from more than one perspective.

After the war ended, and particularly in the last forty years, historians have argued over the real meaning of the battle of El Alamein; this is in fact their duty, since historians should analyse events (also taking hindsight into account) to put them into a more complicated, multi-faceted reality that weighs up all the facts, either known or unknown, at the time the events took place. There have been many criticisms, and in all of them there is at least a grain of truth. If we consider that, according to some authors, the battle of El Alamein should not have been fought at all, it is hard not to say that such a criticism is based on good reasons.

47. After the fall of Tobruk the Axis forces made large use of captured vehicles; a German 20mm anti-aircraft gun mounted on a British 15cwt Bedford lorry.

In fact, it is quite clear that with the Allied invasion of French North-West Africa Rommel might have been compelled to withdraw his forces from Alamein, on the very simple ground that his supply bases would have been directly threatened, and the battle might have been fought some place else without the hindrances and the difficulties of the Axis defence lines and minefields. Yet such a criticism, meaningful and reasonable as it is, is not free from a few flaws; there was no assurance, in the first place, that Rommel might have been compelled to withdraw, for the very simple reason that his forces were simply too far away from Tunisia and thus unable to intervene in any case. Since, as it did in fact happen, the Axis might have built a bridgehead in Tunisia to prevent its seizure from the Allies. Indeed, doubts may arise as to whether Rommel would have been authorised at all to withdraw his forces from Alamein (and one should keep Hitler's order to 'stand fast' in mind in this regard).

Why the Battle was Won

There is also another point well worthy of further discussion; it is certainly true that to face Rommel's army when and where it could take advantage of the defences built at El Alamein was a disadvantage for the Allied forces, with men having to open the way across minefields to fight an enemy well dug in to its defensive line; however, the opposite i.e. an open, fluid battle

48. Rommel with a group of Italian and German officers; cooperation between the Axis forces was always troublesome in the Western Desert.

would also have been a disadvantage. The Germans, and to some extent all the Axis forces in the Western Desert, already had on many occasions proved their superiority when fighting battles in the open ground, where they could take full advantage of their supremacy in the fields of flexibility and manoeuvreability against the British, Commonwealth, Imperial and Dominion forces. There had been just too many cases in the past, last but not least a few months before at Gazala and Tobruk, when the numerically superior forces of the Eighth Army had been defeated simply because the Germans fully exploited the tactical advantages they had on the battleground. One should simply try and imagine what if the second battle of El Alamein had been fought reversing the two sides: the Germans facing Eighth Army's attacks on a terrain of their choice, closer to their supply sources and, above all, not being pressed at all by the need to restore a defence line. Even though this is simply a matter of educated guesswork, one can easily come to the conclusion that the advantages given to Rommel and to his soldiers by the defences at El Alamein could hardly be matched by the advantages both would have really enjoyed if given freedom of manoeuvre and shorter (and more reliable) supply lines.

This leads directly to just another, if not the other, main criticism of the Alamein battle; which is how the battle was fought, or more precisely how Montgomery fought it. There are good reasons behind these criticisms; to sum up in a few words the overall style of command, tactics and doctrine of Field Marshal Montgomery it is easy to say that he was one good step ahead of the Allied commanders on the Western Front in 1918. His set-piece battles, fought with a strict top-down command system on the basis of detailed plans and with the generous support of every available kind of firepower, although successful they might have been, were the direct descendant of those battles fought in the last stage of the First World War, but were also millions of miles away from the evolution that the German Army had brought into mechanised warfare since May 1940. In fact, he was hardly ever able to match the performances of his enemy when the battlefield turned into a fluid one, without defence lines, facing the need to improvise and make concerted use of the initiative. However, this was to be Montgomery's key to the success at El Alamein; even though he managed to largely improve the conditions of his own units, he was perfectly aware of the differences that existed on the actual performances between the Eighth Army and Rommel's Panzer Army Africa. Therefore, the decision to fight at Alamein in a way which compelled Rommel to use his own tactics and doctrine (of counterattacking the enemy to prevent a breakthrough) in a way that turned them into an advantage for the Eighth Army, eventually proved decisive and largely contributed to success on the battlefield.

Criticisms

This does not mean, on the other hand, there were no shortcomings or problems at all; the fact that the remnants of Rommel's army could escape from El Alamein and withdraw all the way to Tripoli and Tunisia does remain a point easy to criticise. Here, too, there are many factors to take into account; on the one hand it is true that Montgomery's forces were largely superior numerically, in particular if we consider the armoured units, and enjoyed a far greater allowance of supplies than those left under Rommel's command did. From this very point of view, Montgomery's excessive use of caution, which one can easily presume was the direct consequence of his lacking both the time and the opportunities to prepare a set-piece battle with an adequate plan and large stocks of supplies, certainly allowed Rommel to evacuate what was left of his Panzer Army Africa back to Tunisia, where it would stand and fight for some three months. Yet, there are other factors to be taken into account; Eighth Army's units were tired and, in many ways, no less worn than their German counterparts since most of the casualties were suffered by the frontline units. Also, the more Rommel withdrew

49. *Field Marshal Bernard Law Montgomery, Viscount of El Alamein, posing after the war in front of the relic of an Italian tank.*

back west, the more the Eighth Army moved away from its own supply sources, which certainly made a full-speed pursuit harder than one can actually imagine. That is without taking into account the changes that were to take place after the end of the battle.

The Turning Point of the Western Desert War

El Alamein was in fact a turning point, from many perspectives. One of its consequences was the change in the balance that so far outlined the composition of the Eighth Army in the Western Desert campaign; since Alamein there were more British than Commonwealth, Imperial and Dominion forces than there had ever been in the Western Desert. After Alamein the latter would shrink even further; the Australian forces, after some two and a half years of battle in the Western Desert, were eventually withdrawn and sent back home. Both the New Zealand and the South African divisions were reorganised, and the role the British units played thereafter became greater and greater. This was a turning point in the British imperial defence system, which would no longer be the same since El Alamein; after Dunkerque, the British Army had eventually been rebuilt and its combat efficiency somehow restored. Since then the main weight of the battle was returned to it, both in Italy and – to a much larger extent – in North-West Europe. The same also happened on the other side; because of the destruction of most of the Italian units at El Alamein, which had supplied the bulk of the Panzer Army Africa infantry, and the eventual withdrawal from the Italian colony of Libya to Tunisia, the last stage of the North African campaign was fought with a greater proportion of German troops than before, and also under direct German control. As it happens, detractors of both the Alamein battle and of Montgomery's command skills have all too often forgotten a key aspect of both the battle and of its aftermath; the role that the destruction of the Italian forces, and the eventual surrender of the last strip of Italian-held land in Africa were to mean for the wider theatre of war.

Well before the disaster of Stalingrad (which many now see as the real turning point of the war), the defeat at Alamein and the events that followed caused a tear in the German–Italian alliance, and it was not mere chance that Italy's eventual invasion and surrender followed less than four months after the end of the North African campaign. Even though the Italians were to lose even more men during the Stalingrad battles than they did at El Alamein, it was eventually the loss of Libya and the bulk of its armoured and mechanised units – not incidentally deployed in the Western Desert – that marked the end of the last combat capabilities (and willingness) of the Italians. And it is not a sheer coincidence that, some seventy years on, Italy is, just like Britain, the one country where the memory of the battle is more vivid and clear than anywhere else, but for quite different reasons.

50. Marching past the wire; all too often the standard battledress or khaki drill uniforms were worn to protect from sand, dust and the night cold.

ORDERS OF BATTLE

Eighth Army (General Bernard Law Montgomery)

XXX Corps (General Oliver Leese)

4th Indian Division (General F.I.S. Tuker)
5th Indian Infantry Brigade, 7th Indian Infantry Brigade, 161st Indian
Infantry Brigade

51st (Highland) Infantry Division (General D.N. Wimberley)
152nd Infantry Brigade, 153rd Infantry Brigade, 154th Infantry Brigade

9th Australian Division (General L.J. Morshead)
20th Australian Infantry Brigade, 24th Australian Infantry Brigade,
26th Australian Infantry Brigade

2nd New Zealand Division (General B.C. Freyberg)
5th New Zealand Infantry Brigade, 6th New Zealand Infantry Brigade,
9th Armoured Brigade (attached)

1st South African Division (General D.H. Pienaar)
1st South African Infantry Brigade, 2nd South African Infantry Brigade,
3rd South African Infantry Brigade

23rd Armoured Brigade Group (Brigadier G.W. Richards)

X Corps (General Herbert Lumsden)

1st Armoured Division (General R. Briggs)
2nd Armoured Brigade, 7th Motor Brigade

10th Armoured Division (General A.H. Gatehouse)
8th Armoured Brigade, 24th Armoured Brigade, 133rd Lorried Infantry Brigade

XIII Corps (General Brian Horrocks)

7th Armoured Division (General A.F. Harding)
4th Light Armoured Brigade, 22nd Armoured Brigade, 131st Infantry Brigade

50th Infantry Division (General J.S. Nichols)
69th Infantry Brigade, 151st Infantry Brigade, 1st Greek Infantry Brigade

44th Infantry Division (General I.T.P. Hughes)
131st Infantry Brigade, 132nd Infantry Brigade

1st Free French Brigade (General P. Koenig)

Panzer Army Africa (General Georg Stumme until 24 October, temporary General Wilhelm von Thoma, since 25 October Field Marshal Erwin Rommel)

Afrika Korps (General Wilhelm von Thoma)

15th Panzer Division (General G. von Vaerst)
(one tank regiment, one motorised infantry regiment, one artillery regiment, one anti-tank battalion, one reconnaissance battalion)

21st Panzer Division (General H. von Randow)
(same as 15th Panzer Division)

90th Light 'Africa' Division (General T. von Sponeck)
(three infantry regiments, one artillery regiment, one anti-tank battalion, one reconnaissance unit)

164th Light 'Africa' Division (General C.H. Lungershausen)
(three infantry regiments, one artillery regiment, one reconnaissance battalion)

Ramcke Luftwaffe Parachute Brigade (General H. Ramcke)

XXI Army Corps – Italian (General E. Navarrini, temporary General A. Gloria)

Infantry Division 'Trento' (General G. Masina)

Infantry Division 'Bologna' (General A. Gloria)

X Army Corps – Italian (General E. Nebbia, temporary General E. Frattini)

Infantry Division 'Brescia' (General B. Brunetti)

Parachute Division 'Folgore' (General E. Frattini)

(attached: Division 'Pavia' (General N. Scattaglia))

XX Army Corps – Italian (General G. De Stefanis)

Armoured Division 'Ariete' (General F. Arena)

Armoured Division 'Littorio' (General G. Bitossi)

Motorised Infantry Division 'Trieste' (General F. La Ferla)

FURTHER READING

Barr, Niall, *Pendulum of War. The Three Battles of El Alamein* (Jonathan Cape, 2004)

Barnett, Corelli, *The Desert Generals* (Ballantine Books, 1960)

Behrendt, Hans Otto, *Rommel's Intelligence in the Desert Campaign* (William Kimber & Co. Ltd,1985)

Bidwell, Shelford and Dominic Graham, *Firepower. British Army Weapons and Theories of War 1904–1945* (HarperCollins Publishers Ltd,1982)

Bungay, Stephen, *Alamein* (Aurum Press Ltd, 2002)

Carell, Paul, The Foxes of the Desert (New English Library, 1961)

Carver, Michael, *El Alamein* (Batsford, 1962)

— *Dilemmas of the Desert War* (John Wiley & Sons,1986)

Churchill, Sir Winston, *The Second World War. Volume 4: The Hinge of Fate* (Cassell & Co., 1951)

De Guingand, Francis, *Operation Victory* (Hodder and Stoughton,1947)

Ellis, John, *Brute Force. Allied Strategy and Tactics in the Second World War* (Andre Deutsch Ltd,1990)

Forty, George, *Afrika Korps at War. Volume 2 – The Long Road Back* (Ian Allan, 1978)

— *Desert Rats at War. North Africa* (Littlehampton Book Services Ltd, 1975)

Fraser, David, *Knight's Cross A Life of Field Marshal Erwin Rommel* (HarperCollins Publishers Ltd, 1993)

French, David, *Raising Churchill's Army. The British Army and the War Against Germany, 1919–1945* (OUP, 2000)

Hamilton, Nigel, *Monty: The Making of a General 1887–1942* (Littlehampton Book Services Ltd, 1982)

Hart, Basil H. Liddell, *The Rommel Papers* (Harcourt, Brace & Co., 1953)

Hinsley, F.H., *et al.*, *British Intelligence in the Second World War: Its Influence on Strategy and Operations. Volume II* (Stationery Office Books, 1984)

Irving, David, *The Trail of the Fox. The Life of Field Marshal Erwin Rommel* (Focal Point Publications, 1977)

Jackson, W.G.F., *The Battle for North Africa* (Mason/Charter Publishers, 1975)

El Alamein 1942

Lucas, James, *War in the Desert. The Eighth Army at El Alamein* (Arms & Armour Press, 1982)

Majdalany, Fred, *The Battle of El Alamein* (Littlehampton Book Services Ltd, 1965)

Maughan, Barton, *Tobruk and El Alamein. Australia in the War of 1939–1945* (Australian War Memorial, 1966)

Montgomery, B.L., *El Alamein to the River Sangro* (Hutchinson, 1948)

Pitt, Barrie, The Crucible of War. Year of Alamein 1942 (Jonathan Cape, 1982)

Playfair, I.S.O., *The Mediterranean and the Middle East. Volume IV: The Destruction of the Axis Forces in Africa* (HMSO, 1966)

Strawson, John, *El Alamein. Desert Victory* (Weidenfeld & Nicholson, 1981)

Walker, Ronald, *Alam Halfa and El Alamein. Official History of New Zealand in the Second World War 1939–45* (Historical Publications Branch, 1967)

There is only one museum dedicated to the battle of El Alamein, located in a marina resort some 65 miles (105km) west of Alexandria. Information on the El Alemein (following Arab spelling) museum can be found at: www. touregypt.net/featurestories/alemeinmuseum.htm

Several museums in the United Kingdom preserve in their collections weapons, vehicles, uniforms, movie footage and memoirs related to the El Alamein battle; the most prominent one is the Imperial War Museum (www.iwm.org.uk) followed by the National Army Museum (www.national-army-museum.ac.uk) and the Royal Artillery Museum (www.firepower.org. uk), all located in the Greater London area. Check the Imperial War Museum website for other related museums located outside London, like Duxford. The Tank Museum, located in Bovington, Dorset (www.tankmuseum.org) is a must for anyone with an interest in tanks and armoured vehicles.

There are not many websites dedicated to the battle of El Alamein, apart from the Wikipedia ones, and the most interesting ones are those of the Australian War Memorial (www.awm.gov.au), which includes official histories and records related to the battle, and the New Zealand collection of official histories, available at the following website: www.nzetc.org/tm/scholarly/subject-000004.html. Worth mentioning is the good website of the BBC (www.bbc.co.uk/history/interactive/animations/wwtwo_map_el_alamein/index_embed.shtml), which includes an animated map.

Strangely enough, no movies about the El Alamein battle were produced in the United Kingdom, or even in Hollywood. The closely related one is Henry Hathaway's 'Rommel. The Desert Fox' (1951), starring James Mason in the title role. On the other hand, the battle provided the background of several Italian movies, mostly low budget ones filmed on entirely different locations. Some are worth seeing: Duilio Coletti's 'Division Folgore' (1955), Guido Malatesta's 'El Alamein' (1957) and Calvin Jackson Padget's French-Italian co-production 'La battaglia di El Alamein' (1969). In 2002 a new movie was released, directed by Enzo Monteleone and entitled 'El Alamein. La linea del fuoco'.

INDEX

Index

EXPLORE HISTORY'S MAJOR CONFLICTS
WITH BATTLE STORY

978-0-7524-6201-1 £9.99

978-0-7524-6196-1 £9.99

978-0-7524-6310-1 £9.99

978-0-7524-6202-1 £9.99

978-0-7524-6311-1 £9.99

978-0-7524-6268-1 £9.99